PUNKER 2 PASTOR

From a Radical Life of Punk Rock to a
Radical Life for Christ

By
Pastor Kelly Lohrke
Senior Pastor of Praise Chapel Christian Fellowship
of Kansas City, Kansas

D1057533

PRESS

Copyright © 2009 by Pastor Kelly Lohrke

Punker 2 Pastor
From a Radical life of Punk Rock to a
Radical life for Christ
by Pastor Kelly Lohrke

Printed in the United States of America

ISBN 9781615791392

All rights reserved solely by the author. The author guarantees all contents are original and do not infringe upon the legal rights of any other person or work. No part of this book may be reproduced in any form without the permission of the author. The views expressed in this book are not necessarily those of the publisher.

Unless otherwise indicated, Bible quotations are taken from
> The N.I.R.V. Copyright © 1998 by Biblica.
> The N.A.S. Copyright © 1995 by The Lockman Foundation.
> The N.K.J. Copyright © 1982 by Thomas Nelson, Inc.

www.xulonpress.com

❧

"Jesus turned water into wine, walked on the water, raised the dead and fed multitudes with a few fish and loaves. The greatest miracle Christ does is when he totally transforms a human being. The Apostle Paul said, "Anyone who believes in Christ is a new creation. The old is going! The new has come!" (2 Corinthians 5:17 NIRV).

That is what happened to Kelly Lohrke.

To call Kelly a "miracle" is no stretch of the word. As you read his personal life story, you will be reminded that, "Nothing is impossible with God." His story will convince you that God loves lost people. This miracle will build your confidence that God can use you and fulfill destiny for your life."

Larry Neville, President
Praise Chapel Christian Fellowship Churches and
Ministries International

• • •

"Kelly's story is like reading a chapter out of the book of Acts. It is filled with excitement, danger and miracles. This book is sure to be an inspiration to all who read it and will surely lead many to faith in Christ."

Dennis Slavens, Senior Pastor
Antioch Church - Kansas City

• • •

"Not only is this one of the most powerful stories in Christianity, it's only the small part of the impact in his life. Pastor Kelly is able to relate to and influence any age culture and heart. As a close friend I've seen him witness to strangers in ways that show the reality of his life and heart. Read this not as a story, but as a life."

Ron Simpkins
Author, Pastor and Conference Speaker

TABLE OF CONTENTS

PART ONE - WIN ONE: THE PUNKER 15

CHAPTER ONE: A Door to the Fury.............17
CHAPTER TWO: The Twist on the Road.......27
CHAPTER THREE: The Education of a
    Degenerate 37
CHAPTER FOUR: The Dance of Slow
    Death...47
CHAPTER FIVE: A Hand in the Fire.............59
CHAPTER SIX: The Final Straw 73

PART TWO - BUILD ONE: THE DISCIPLE.......83

CHAPTER ONE: Unhooking from the Fury...85
CHAPTER TWO: The Making of a
    Preacher..107
CHAPTER THREE: Training for Life 129
CHAPTER FOUR: Answering the Call.........159

PART THREE - SEND ONE: THE PASTOR 171

CHAPTER ONE: The Road to Destiny.........173
CHAPTER TWO: Life as a Pioneer 185
CHAPTER THREE: The Other Kansas
        City...203
CHAPTER FOUR: Moments in the
        Spotlight..221
CHAPTER FIVE: Going Places 241

AUTHOR'S NOTE

This is a true story. The names of some of the people have been changed to protect their identities. The places and companies that Pastor Kelly worked at, visited or mentioned are part of his story and in no way reflect how these places or companies are today.

INTRODUCTION

*O*nly *five hundred dollars! One man's dream and another man's destiny are forever altered. It began with a mailman named Bobby. With his lease almost up, he desperately needed to move. Long hours at the post office did not permit him to look for a place to stay. The $500 that he had saved was barely enough for him and his family to move.*

It was a normal Wednesday. For Bobby, that meant going to church. He happened to carry his $500 in his pocket. There were no special offerings that day. Yet as the offering plate passed by, he felt the Lord tell him to put in the whole $500! Without hesitation, he tossed it in, obeying the Lord completely.

His wife asked him, "What are you doing?"

He told her that he felt God speak to him to put the $500 in the offering. Their house money now gone, the couple went home that night and prayed that the Lord would bless their family.

Bobby had a dream as he slept that night. In this dream he saw a house, its color, the landscape and everything. Halfway through his delivery route the next day, Bobby saw the house that was in his dream. This was unbelievable! He was certain that this was the house he saw in his dream because everything matched. There was no "for sale" or "for rent" signs posted. Upon closer inspection of the house he found that it was empty.

Seeing that the neighbors were home, he went and asked them about the house. He was told that an elderly couple owned it but had retired and moved two hours out of town. Using the neighbors' phone, he called the owner. He explained that he was the mailman and noticed that the house was empty, and he was inquiring about it. The owner seemed very friendly and offered to drive the two hours to meet with Bobby in front of the house after work.

Later when they met, the old man asked, "So, how much money do you have?"

Taking a deep breath, Bobby replied, "None."

The owner, who had a puzzled and upset look on his face, replied "You made me drive all this way and you have no money?"

Bobby explained that he saw this house in a dream and he believed that the Lord wanted him to live in it.

"You're crazy!" said the old man "But I'll call my wife."

He went to the neighbors' house to use the phone and came back out saying, "I don't know why I'm doing this, but here are the keys."

Bobby and his wife Melinda moved in and lived in the house for several years. During this time, they served in the church, became leaders and soon were sent out to pioneer a church. They were such good tenants that when Bobby called the owner to thank him and to tell him that they were moving out to start a church, the owner was not eager to lose them.

"You took such good care of my house," the old man responded. "Is there anybody in your church like you that I can trust to move in my house?"

Bobby had a couple of people in mind: his brother, Albert and his wife Yolanda!

"There is one catch," the owner revealed. "I have a grandson that is messed up on drugs and people are after him. He needs help. Do you think they'd let him live in the garage?"

Bobby and Albert agreed. A few months later, a jeep pulled up in the driveway and out came; a tall, skinny, junkie-looking kid with blue-black spiked hair. He was wearing a leather jacket and combat boots up to his knees, and he looked completely wasted on drugs.

When Albert and Yolanda saw him, they thought, "What have we gotten ourselves into?"

I was that junkie-looking kid who stepped out of that jeep. And so, here is the rest of my story.

PART ONE

WIN ONE: THE PUNKER

CHAPTER ONE

A Door to the Fury

Hook on the Jaw

A part from the soft thud of my shoes on the threshold, the house was silent. Tossing my backpack on the couch, I pocketed the door key as I slammed the door shut. Robotically I reached for the television knob, the sure noisemaker in the house, and yanked up the volume. I followed my stomach to the kitchen for an after school-snack. The fridge and cupboards had enough food for more than two people. A gnawing that could not be ignored arose again and for a brief moment, I suffered from a latch key kid's enemy – loneliness.

Being an only child and growing up in a single parent home had its bad side effects. Dad abandoned mom and me when I was only six weeks old. Although it was difficult for me to grow up without a father, my mom was spared from the beatings my dad would give her in the past. Sadly, the other men that came into my mom's life were no better, for some did resort to abusing her too. Consequently, mom never remarried and I remained the only child.

A daughter of one of the founders of a very successful company called Aerospace Aluminum Heat Treatment Company (a producer of many parts for the United States space shuttles), mom grew up in a wealthy home and was apparently spoiled. Yet, she was determined to be independent. So she became a hard working single mom, and I ended up a latchkey son, at ten years old.

Living in a well-to-do suburb of Southeast Los Angeles, California, in the 1970s and early 1980s was no shelter from the destruction that lured me in at a young age. All the material things that my grandparents and mom gave me could not buy what I wanted most; an escape from the pain of loneliness. Often, I wanted a dad at home or siblings, and even friends to fill that emptiness. For me, that became the set up for the fast and furious track drawing me toward destruction. But before the chaos began in my life, an opportunity to escape it came.

Movies and church did not really mix – at least not in those days. This was about 1980 or 1981. But a movie in church was enough to peak my curiosity. Urged by my cousin, I reluctantly went with my dad and my stepfamily to see the *Thief in the Night*. God and church were not realities that I cared about or wanted in my life.

For the next few hours, I sat through a terrifying presentation of the Gospel. That night, my young mind translated the message of the movie as if I did not receive Jesus as my savior, my head was going to be chopped off. My only chance to avoid that fate was the whisking away of all Christians in something called the "rapture." If I took what was termed the "mark of the beast" to save my neck, I would be thrown into the eternal lake of fire or hell. In the end, I lifted up my hand to get "saved" and I followed the many people to the altar when Pastor Jeff Johnson of Downey Calvary Chapel invited people to receive Jesus into their lives. A prayer in the back room with some people sealed my decision that night. This marked the beginning of many tormenting flashbacks in a lifestyle that I later chose.

Church was part of dad's family, so I was dragged to it for two months. What took two months to establish was destroyed in one day, or so I thought. Upon returning to my mom's house, the news had gotten around that I was going to a "born again church." I heard an old friend saying this when I went back to junior high school and figured this leak came from my mom. Somehow, I was embarrassed to have my friends know that I went to church. Not wanting to be labeled as "one of those," I decided to distance myself from that rumor. I chose then not to serve God.

The decision not to serve God may have been something I made in my heart, but my body followed it with full force. Within a short time, I had manifested all sorts of destructive behaviors that were fueled by constantly partying with my friends and diving deeper into drugs. But the hook was already set.

Fostering the Enemy

The ecstasy was indescribable. It was like a burst of energy that surged through me promising a never-ending life in fantasyland, something that I had been looking for. I loved the way I felt – no cares, no fears and definitely none of that lonely pain that filled my life for such a long time. Nothing bothered me. Not even the fact that the cupboards and fridge were empty and the overflowing trashcan showed that I had fed all our groceries to my hungry friends. In my clenched fist were the speed pills and my ticket to the temporary and powerful emotional lift.

It had been over two and a half years since I became a latchkey kid. My friends were now regulars at my house after school. A few months before, some of them had introduced me to their parents' and older brothers' other preoccupations – taking and selling drugs. Television and playing pool were no longer enough to fill our extended hours of boredom and emptiness. Growing older must have been a factor in our change of appetite for entertainment and use of our time. I could not deny the fact that my amazing first high from taking drugs was like a bottomless pit that called, "Feed me!" We all took the bait. Drugs were now part of our hanging out and sleepovers, with our samplings ranging from weed, Christmas trees[1] and speed pills. I was now about twelve years old and changing extremely fast.

Being a suburban kid, I was able to support my new habit. Some of my friends were not so fortunate, and had to fight to get money for the drugs. At the same time, I was becoming defiant and increasingly rebellious. I began to experience an emotional bareness and a greater separation toward my mother. Mom did not know what to do with me. Reacting violently to whatever irked me was too much for her. Her temporary solution was to try to give me away.

Dad was first on her list. Living with my dad was miserable in more ways than one. Not only did I resist making that arrangement permanent, I hated the whole situation. My dad was like a stranger, who was trying to get to know me, and I wanted no part of it. He also put somewhat of a damper on my drug habit. Perhaps subconsciously I was afraid of the man. He had not hesitated to give my face a forceful taste of his knuckles, busting my braces, for calling him a "baby." Layer that on top of the frequent animated spats between him and mom where I was the pawn; it was a role that I soon came to resent.

Mom exhausted all her possible sources of homes for me. My aunt and uncle could only tolerate me briefly. Their desire to protect my younger cousins from my unruly behavior outweighed their wanting to help out my mom. A stay with another cousin was almost as short-lived as the previous living arrangements. Finally, in another desperate effort, mom

---

[1] Marijuana; amphetamine; methamphetamine; depressant

sent me to another aunt and uncle. That move was no different from the others since I was back home within a short time. No one seemed to want me, including my mom. All I could figure out at the time was that if she did not want me, then it was up to me to find love elsewhere. Anger, loneliness and rejection fed that conclusion. Mom and I grew further apart and the unpleasant tension grew. Not long after that, I hit her. That tore her life apart.

Hitting mom was a natural progression on the maddening road that I was traveling at the time. There were advantages to being taller at fourteen years old than the woman who bore me. I found that I could shut her up quicker by towering over her and shouting obscenities in her face whenever she made me mad. This came to a head one morning as she drove me to school. I was in eighth grade and I was in trouble with the school. In her frustration with my latest school offenses, mom was yelling at me. By then, I was quite skilled in tuning out her outbreaks. My defiant and uncaring attitude must have been obvious, for mom was unable to contain her anger any longer and she hit me. Something in me snapped as I felt a rage coming up from deep within me and I hit her back. She slapped me again and I returned the favor, only harder. Mom's ability to discipline me was muted forever that day. Discipline had come too late.

Efforts at patching our tattered relationship were futile. An emotional death in our relationship was pulling us further apart. Hanging out with friends consumed most of my life and mom hardly saw me anymore. Being with my friends and their families was a better trade than what my home offered. Mom was kept in the dark about the drugs even though I was already dropping acid at this point. Naturally, my role models then were some of my friends and their families. Seeing my friends openly smoke opium, for instance, or take some other drug with the full knowledge of their parents, especially in their own house, was appealing to me. I thought this was pretty cool! Why not me? When one mom commented that she was "glad" that her "son was open" with her about using drugs, the idea in my head turned into a plan. It seemed possible that letting mom in on my secret that I was using drugs would reduce the strain in our relationship. No one and nothing in the world prepared me for the outcome of that decision.

Pulling out my bed, I retrieved all my drugs from their hiding place in the corner. Everything was laid out neatly on my bed. Then I waited.

Mom was barely home from work on that fateful day when I approached her and said, "Mom, I want to talk to you."

Eager to reveal my forbidden collection, I led my mother to my room. She may have suspected that I took drugs, but not to the extent that laid before her eyes.

"Mom, this is my *bong!*"[2] I explained with a smile on my face and feeling proud that I was finally being honest with her. Then like a pro, I began to

---

[2] Drug paraphernalia

show her the drugs and paraphernalia, and even how I rolled weed!

Her only response was, "Oh my God!"

Within twenty-four hours, my mother had me arrested and I was on my way to the Charter Baywood mental facilities. It seemed like my mom got rid of me in a panic. I was only fourteen years old at the time. And so began my journey that seemed more like a version of the song "Institutionalized" by Suicidal Tendencies.

Fatherless Generation

It is amazing, the role of fathers in the lives of their children. Though the world seeks to eliminate and downplay the importance of fathers in the homes, reality cries out that societal ills hinge on this one truth – children need fathers. Sadly, this is becoming more and more a fatherless generation.

A father in a child's formative years is crucial because the home is where a child develops a sense of identity and a proper relationship to God. The way a child relates to his or her father later translates into either a healthy or an unhealthy view of God as a father. Children need the leadership of their fathers.

Statistics show that fatherlessness is "the most significant family or social problem facing America." *Fatherless homes have yielded these results: 85% of youths in prisons, 80% of children who commit rape, and children at high risk for drug and alcohol* *addictions. Also it was found that 63% of fatherless children had "subjective psychological problems (defined as anxiety, sadness, pronounced moodiness, phobias, and depression)*. These are sobering realities to a growing problem, one to which I attest.*

*www.lifecoaches.org, www.fathers.com, www. childrensjustice.org, www.religionandsocialpolicy. org, www.pewresearch.org, National Center for Fathering, Fathering in America Poll, January 1999.

CHAPTER TWO

The Twist on the Road

Institutionalized: I'm Not Crazy!

Stripped of my clothes, the hospital gown hung on me loosely, except where the straitjacket had me in a death grip. I awoke and realized that this was no illusion. Pink padded walls stared at me from the steel room. The bed held me fast in a five-point restraint. Drugged. I felt the staff's coming and going in a perpetual daze. This drug-induced high at the facility was greater than any high that I had known. And I was helpless against the staff's freedom to inject me with drugs whenever they wanted. Thoughts swam through my head in that hazy world. How could my mom do this to me – turn me over to a mental institution? Humiliation and confusion simply mocked me.

Days passed in the pink room. Days where I imagined that this was just a bad dream that would soon evaporate and I would wake up in my own bed. But the endless nightmare continued. Being released to a regular room was a step up from the pit. I had a punker for a roommate! Punk rock was our love and passion and so we hit it off. The dreadful stay became slightly tolerable, at least until the eight weeks I was promised at the mental hospital were up. But all I could think about was getting out of there.

It was the eighth week and I was sitting across from the psychiatrist. Such a blah moment! Everything she said did not seem to register until she dropped the bombshell — my stay at the hospital was extended. That cut me deeply. All my hatred for that place seeped out in protest. Liars! Betrayal! Anger took over and I cussed her out mercilessly. My ranting and raving did not change anything except draw eight staffers from the cold hallways. The vigilant pack circled around her door as I stormed out of her office.

"Calm down!" one of them cautioned and others mumbled similar phrases and all the while, their palms were opened, ready to pounce.

Clearly cornered and outnumbered, they cried in unison, "Get him!"

Within moments, I was restrained and carted off to the pink steel trap. They shot me with a drug and kept me in there for three days. I may have been calm on the outside but a raging rebellion was solidifying inside me.

Disturbing happenings at the facility also began to feed my deep-seated anger. The facility was coed and housed both adults and juveniles. Dark memories and images from those months ate at me: like the time the kid in the next room cut his wrist with a lightbulb and blood splattered everywhere. Or seeing adult staff members kissing and messing around with teenagers housed in the facility. Many times the staff allowed the teenage boys to take showers with girls and that led to many sexual experiences. Being disciplined a few days later by the staff for such behaviors were confusing – they encouraged them in the first place.

Promises of being released early were made by the staff many times. They would enter my room and say, "Lohrke, you are getting out tomorrow." My excitement would be crushed the next day when it did not happen. The disappointments kept turning into anger especially when they laughed it off as a joke.

Drugs were also readily supplied by some staffers to hospital patients, including weekend passes to meet them in their homes for drugs, parties and sex. I was not exempt from these corruptions and violations. Any innocence that remained in my life was completely destroyed in that facility. I experienced more abuse, sex, drugs, perversion and all kinds of evil than I ever had growing up outside of those walls.

Spending more weeks and months at the facility was bad, but staying in there that Christmas and New Year's was worse. Holidays usually produced good memories, but that year, I had none. Unknowingly, mom was dishing out money to an institution that failed to help me – rather it was slowly killing me inside.

Brief Breakaways

Hope for freedom came to me in weird ways. Escape was a better alternative to being slowly institutionalized. Another kid and I forged an escape plan. Somehow, we persuaded the janitor to leave the back door next to the lounge area unlocked. At about 8:30 that night, our opportunity came swiftly. The staff turned their backs for a few minutes and we sprung through that door and ran. Sprinting down the long driveway, we clambered over an iron fence, turned the corner on Paramount Boulevard and dove into the first bush we saw. Four hours inched by. Convinced that they could not catch us in the darkness, our pursuers (the police and the staffers) surrendered us to the night. It was midnight when we began the thirty-mile trek toward our only destination — my grandparents' house.

They will understand and let me stay, I thought.

But any hope for compassion was squelched at sunup when we arrived. Grandpa and Grandma refused my begging and pleading. That letdown from my grandparents really hurt. They simply handed me over to the staff that came to fetch me. I was hospital property.

The flimsy hospital gown replaced my dispossessed clothes. Secured once again in the pink cell, I was also placed on suicide watch. But I had no desire to die. I just wanted out. I was a drug addict and not an insane suicidal lunatic!

More crazy treatment followed. Assured that I was subdued, I was transferred to the high-security ward reserved for troubled people. This was utter madness to me. I felt caged. Depression had a choke-hold on me, and I succumbed to it. For three weeks, I sat in silence, staring out of the barred window. It seemed as if life existed only outside the walls of the hospital.

Everything changed when Mike Camp entered my room. He looked at me, walked over and jumped on his bed. His declaration was believably bold.

"I'm not going to be in here with a sad, depressed kid!" he said. "We're going to get out of here!"

It worked.

The fog of depression vaporized. I had caught a glimpse of freedom…again.

Mike was my new roommate and a well-known escapee within the facility. The staff had reluctantly paired him up with me because overcrowding gave them no other alternative. Their fears were not unfounded, for shortly afterward, Mike and I had hatched another escape plan.

Every step of the breakout was planned until we were sure it would work. Execution day came and we were ready. Stolen shorts and T-shirt under-neath my hospital gown clung to my skin as Mike and I awaited our "escape" cue. Mike had fished the clothes from behind the counter when the front desk was momentarily unmanned. Our cue to escape came from a deafening noise over the loudspeaker. A punk rock song drowned out Mike's karate chop of the back door's deadbolt lock. As we tore out of there, a girl who was just as eager to leave followed us out. Dodging in and out of every third house, we wove our way down the street straight into a cul-de-sac.

Trapped.

Our hearts were pounding because we knew that the police and the van with the restraints were coming down the street. Feeling boxed in, we turned toward the house with the blaring rock music. Several Harleys were parked in front. That could only mean…a party! And our only hope of a hiding place!

We pounded on the door. A biker chick answered our desperate thumps.

She took one look and announced, "Oh! The crazy kids are here! Come on in!"

The bikers hid us. We partied the night away with them, happily burning our hospital gowns in return for different clothes. Still high the next morning, the bikers drove us to Mike's parents' house nearby in Redondo Beach. Empty. Mike's parents were in Europe. This became our perfect hideout for two days.

On the second day, there was a sharp rap on the door. Mike answered and saw cops standing there. They were looking for a "Kelly Lohrke."

"No, there's no Kelly here," Mike replied nonchalantly.

He continued to lie, "I'm the only one here!"

Incidentally, I was in the living room talking to my grandma on the phone (I was just telling her that

I was fine) and in plain sight and earshot of the police at the door.

"Well, who is that?" asked one of the cops pointing at me.

A few minutes later, I was arrested and escorted to a police car. Mike was picked up a while later only after the cops received a call from the station asking if they got the "blonde kid"(Mike) too. I was put in jail. But as a hospital patient, they checked me out of that prison and I went back into the mental facility.

Not long after that, my mom's insurance ran out and I was released from the hospital. They termed my release as having "graduated." Eight long, hellish months had passed. I had turned fifteen. But I was worse than I had ever been.

Releasing Restraints

"Immediately a man from the tombs with an unclean spirit met Him, and he had his dwelling among the tombs. And no one was able to bind him anymore, even with a chain; because he had often been bound with shackles and chains, and the chains had been torn apart by him and the shackles broken in pieces, and no one was strong enough to subdue him (Mark 5:1-5 NAS)."

I found myself in this story. Centuries may separate our lives but our experiences were similar – we were bound and hated it. Just noting our common ground was comforting. Society had us isolated for "our own good" and the safety of other people. They picked the tombs for the demoniac, and I ended up at the mental hospital. Chained to the tombs, he managed to break and smash those constraints occasionally and had to be restrained many times over. My momentary flights to freedom were rewarded with the straitjacket and pink cell.

Stronger chains, isolation, and straitjackets do not equate with freedom, nor do they soothe internal torments. Constant human efforts to tame either of us did not work but only strengthened the desire to be free. Rebellion against those restraints and attempts to help us were almost inevitable.

Places of restraint may have been different, but each was lonely. Tombs represent dead people and the demoniac lived among the tombs many times; the mental hospital felt like a place for the dead to me. Evil roamed there, unleashing uncomfortable moments of darkness. That institution was my lonely place.

For the demoniac, it was in that lonely place where he cried out and cut himself with stones (Mark 5:5). Out of his right mind, he was slowly destroying his body. Abusing drugs and using needles to shoot my veins for a high after I got out of the institution was like gashing myself with sharp rocks. That self-destructive desire was alive in my mind. What I cried out for was a savior to give me true liberty.

It was a good day when the demoniac met Jesus. Tormented by the presence of the Savior, the crying out got Jesus' attention. He heard and saw the condition of the demoniac and with a command, the oppressed man was freed forever. Jesus heard my crying out too, and gave me true freedom. From that day, a desire to follow the true liberator was born in that man, just as it became true for me (Mark 5:6-8).

> *"And coming out, the unclean spirits entered the swine; and the herd rushed down the steep bank into the sea, about two thousand of them; and they were drowned in the sea. Their herdsmen ran away and reported it in the city and in the country. And the people came to see what it was that had happened. They came to Jesus and observed the man who had been demon-possessed sitting down, clothed and in his right mind, the very man who had had the "legion"; and they became frightened. Those who had seen it described to them how it had happened to the demon-possessed man, and all about the swine. And they began to implore Him to leave their region (Mark 5:11-17)."*

But not everyone celebrated this man's newfound liberty. Seeing the demoniac in his right mind was a fearful thing for them. Unable to comprehend the touch of God, those who knew the man's past reacted with fear and anger to his true freedom. Was it for real? What could it mean? Fear and uncertainty eventually overcame them so that they could not share the joy of this man's deliverance. The owners of the pigs were not happy – they lost their pigs!

Even today, there are those who are unwilling to pay the price to see others saved, especially if it costs them something. In my case, my family members were happy at first when Jesus delivered me. Then, they became unhappy because I was at church all the time. But that is jumping ahead in the story!

****

CHAPTER THREE

The Education of a Degenerate

School on the Rocks

"Every time I see you in here, I will give you two spankings."

Unfortunately for me, the junior-high principal delivered on that promise. Totally preoccupied with peddling drugs and doing foul things, being a good student was not a priority. Curbing my bad behavior must have been a headache for the principal and one particular teacher, Mr. Jones (not his real name). He was a tormentor. A dread. Spanking me daily was his way of dealing with me. Until one day, when I could not handle it anymore and quit school.

"I'm out of here!" I announced.

But it was hard to be a dropout at junior high so I managed to get into high school.

I was a student embracing the crazy motto "A friend with weed is a friend indeed." I lived it. And the connections that opened up were of the deadly kind. Someone introduced me to a needle. Call it my "divine appointment with the devil." Cocaine and heroin had found me at fifteen.

Defiant behaviors increased as I fried my brains on drugs. The school's patience soon ran out and I was kicked out after multiple trips to the principal's office. By a miracle, I enrolled at Downey High School. But my dread followed. Mr. Jones, that junior high school teacher who enjoyed beating me, became a teacher at my new school. Still, he was the least of my worries.

Punk rock had me in a headlock. It drew me like a nail to a magnet. But it fit me like a glove. And so my clothes, hairstyle, body piercing and wicked tattoos represented that subculture. Anger had festered in me to such a degree that when I came out of that mental institution, punk rock expressed outwardly my inner rage. The high school did not take too kindly to my punk rocker assortment. On the first day, I was sent home.

"Your hair has too many colors." I was told.

My hair was dyed in "fruit loop" colors with green and yellow shades. The expulsion from the other school was still fresh in my mind. Cooperating somewhat would keep me in. Reluctantly, I got my hair down to one shade. It was not all that the school found offensive.

"You have too many earrings!" Okay, I could handle that, I thought. I removed the extra earrings.

Walking into school the next day wearing my bondage pants (the legs were tied together), I violated the dress code. That was too much for me.

"Forget you!" I shouted, "I ain't coming back to this stupid school!"

I kept my word. And for sometime, I was free of the watchful eye of Mr. Jones.

Being a high school dropout did not last long. A friend told me about continuation school. I understood this as a school where students went after expulsion from all the other schools.

"We are overtaking it with punkers," he reported with some enthusiasm. "We need you." Now I was listening.

He explained, "You only have to go to school until noon. And you work at your own pace (which is practically none at all) and most of all, you can sell drugs and get away with it." That was the clincher. I was in.

Continuation school was another avenue to increase my drug sales. Everything else seemed an insignificant blur. Attempts by people in the school to help me were merely ignored or dismissed.

Once the principal called me into the office and remarked, "You look sick."

I lied, "No, I'm all right."

He insisted with a knowing expression, "No, you look sick."

Any onlooker could tell that I was physically ill. Hepatitis was turning my eyes, nails and skin yellow. I guessed the day I got it. A friend of mine had drugs and a syringe with a little blood on it. He had picked it up from somewhere. None of us knew whose blood it was nor did we care. A quick rinse later, it was embedded in my arm. It came on sometime after that — hepatitis in full force. I was sixteen years old. But there was no way I was going to admit that to the principal.

Lessons of Another Kind

I was a student of drugs and punk rock. My life and relationships revolved around these loves. Home was a popular hangout for my friends – even when I was not home. Waiting for me at my house with stolen stuff to hock for money was not uncommon. I had developed shady connections. This constant influx of activity at my house was scary for my mom and our neighbors in this suburban neighborhood. Mom's decision to turn into her driveway depended on whether she saw signs of my friends at our house or not. More often than not, she kept right on driving. I was too strung out to care. We had pretty much taken over the house.

Hunger for a fix was the monster that drove me. Trafficking drugs as a student was one way to feed the beast that was growing inside of me. Any avenue that opened up for business I kept milking for more money — like my bedroom window. Known as "the window," this convenient spot was frequented by colorful visitors: Mexican gang members, older guys and even prisoners. Business was open at all hours of the day and night. Raking in large amounts of money from drug sales at fifteen was enough to keep me drooling for more. A sheet of acid was about $250 and there were one hundred hits a sheet, with five dollars a hit. I made about $250. But that was only a trickle in the dirty stream.

The gush came through a biker friend of my dad's. He offered to take me to a place where I could make an eye-popping amount. Called Haight-Ashbury in California, it was a hang out for '60s hippies and Timothy Leary.[3] There, I got my hands on twenty pure LSD sheets for $30 each. I later sold them for $470 a sheet! That day, I became a drug runner between San Francisco, Los Angeles and Orange County in California. The profitable income drew me from Los Angeles to San Francisco every two weeks, with sheets of acid accompanying my luggage on the airplanes. I contributed to the ravenous market for acid in the Los Angeles and Orange County clubs.

All kinds of evil were now accessible to me. I truly experienced what the scriptures say that the love of money is the root to all kinds of evil. Having that kind of money at such a young age exposed me to hanging out with older men and women who were very experienced with drugs and all kinds of perversion. I found myself shooting up drugs and performing many perverted sexual acts with older women. Money drove me to all the drugs, sex and parties I desired. Though money came and went, my

---

[3] He was an American writer and pyschologist who was an advocate of psychedelic drug research. Also an icon of 1960s counterculture, Leary was most famous as a proponent of the therapeutic, spiritual and emotional benefits of LSD.

drug craving never did. It consumed every penny I made.

Robbery was an easy step down for my friends and me. Looting, plundering homes and getting guns were all part of it. Once we started robbing people, it was hard to stop. I was busted immediately after the first robbery for receiving stolen property that I told my friends to steal. Blue hair was my dead give-away too. While high on acid one day, I got a call from some younger punkers who committed many robberies. They said that they were at a house and needed a car to pick up the stuff. In a red convertible VW bus, my friends and I pulled up and robbed that house at midday — as the neighbors watched! The cops came and arrested me at the continuation school.

"Have you ever done this before?" the police asked.

"No" I confessed, "this is my first time."

"Don't do it again," they advised and then released me.

But the police were back at the continuation school the next week. I had committed another robbery. I saw them coming. Knowing they were looking for me, I hid in the bathroom. I was arrested a second time while on probation.

That was when I ran into none other than Mr. Jones again. He had become a teacher at the continuation school. Was he following me? His toleration of me came to an abrupt end one day.

"Lohrke, you see that gate?" he said pointing to the school entrance. "Your school days are over. I want you to just walk out of that gate and never come back. This is your last stop. Don't worry about the paperwork; I'll take care of it."

He was dead serious. And so was I. For me, school was officially over.

On My Own

Smoke and the stench of drugs leaked out from my bedroom. About seven of my friends and I were getting loaded in there. Somewhere in my house, my two sets of grandparents waited for me to join them in celebrating my sixteenth birthday. They were over at my house with a birthday cake to celebrate my special day. Drugs had fried my brains to the point where common courtesy and respect were foreign concepts to me.

When my grandfathers could not wait anymore, one of them knocked on my door and said, "Can I please talk to you?"

Reluctantly, I staggered down to the front porch where my German grandpas (both named Fred) began to talk to me. No, they were not willing to sit idly by and see me destroy my life. They told me that I was going to get out of there and I was going to live with them...an offer that was met by a stream of obscenities, from me.

"You ain't gonna make me do nothing!" I protested and dragged myself back to my room.

Moments later, the wrath of the old men came, preceded by the bedroom door being kicked open. Whatever my grandpas were about to unleash, none of my friends wanted any piece of it. Terror-stricken, they all bailed out the window. I'd never seen a room empty so fast. One of the two Freds locked the window.

"You want to go through that window too?" one grandpa bellowed.

Not waiting for me to smart back, he picked me up, threw me against the closed window and then tossed me back onto the bed. Instantly, one of them was holding me down while the other went into a ballistic old man rage, punching me mercilessly.

"Hit him, Freddy!" one urged, while the other hollered back, "Hold him, Freddy!" This went on for quite a while, each man encouraging the other to pummel me full of fists. When the old men's anger was spent, they lifted me up and shoved me out of my bedroom window. I gathered myself up, brushed off the shards of glass from my clothes and figured I was now on my own.

Still bleeding with cuts and bruises from the beating and being thrust through the window, I limped down to the liquor store followed by my friends. Getting loaded was the memory killer for a lousy birthday party. Making drugs out of cough syrup was our plan.

But my eye caught sight of a punker girl who I had met earlier that week at a thrift store. She was at the liquor store. Propriety was not something I practiced. One meeting was all I needed before I had gone home with one of her friends (even though she lived hours away from me). The punker girl's eyes widened when she saw me all bloodied and beat up.

"What happened?" she asked.

"I was just thrown out of my house. I got nowhere to go," I replied.

"We just got an apartment down the street," she said.

Then her voice softened, "Come live with us." I did not need a second invitation.

That same day, I moved in with these older punker girls, who were a part of a gang called the Los Angeles Death Squad (LADS – a hardcore punker gang known for being a very violent group). I pitched in by helping these women make and use LSD and PCP. It lasted about a year.

Getting my own apartment came about a year later. One of the women I lived with received a one-year lease of an apartment plus ten thousand dollars as the bride price from an illegal Chinese guy. She was his ticket into the United States. Already with an apartment, the lady gave me the newly leased apartment for free.

My punker friends and I moved in and we destroyed the place. Parties were constant occurrences. Girls frequented the apartment. We dealt drugs and smoked them like there was no tomorrow. We were so bad that at Christmastime, we ripped off fifteen Christmas trees from the grocery store across the street and just stuffed them into the apartment. It looked like a forest in there – and it was not because we had any use for those trees.

Sometime later, I heard that one of my grandpas had died. Coincidently, something had made me so angry that I took a handful of Valium pills. I had learned that anger and rebellion could be masked with a high – and Valium pills were available.

I woke up to my dad hitting me. Tubes were coming out of my nose and attached to my arm. This rude awakening was more than what I wanted.

"What are you doing?" he asked.

Why does he care? I thought. *He had not been there for me before.*

"Get out!" was all I muttered.

Waking up in a hospital bed filled in the missing details. I had overdosed. Mom thought it was in response to my grandpa's death. But I knew it was more out of anger and rebellion than having a death wish. Thankfully, God had saved my bacon to live another day.

CHAPTER FOUR

The Dance of Slow Death

Reveling in Punk Rock

Spiked with egg whites, my dyed hair stood still even when I yanked and banged my head to the music. The leather jacket boasting patches of past concerts I'd conquered and my knee-high combat boots blended well with the dancing mass of similarly dressed bodies. Hurling myself off the stage onto the swirling crowd, the exhilaration energized me for more of this madness. I screamed, punched and pushed closer to the stage. I was going to jump again. This was punk rock and I was a punk rocker. I loved it!

I was a child of the '80s. Trends that marked this era put a stamp on me as well. MTV was born. Hair spray was a big deal. Everyone seemed to have hairspray or hair gel, even the jocks! Music as a major way of expression for the young people took on new meaning. Young people began to identify their lives and clothing with their choice of music. Kids in my generation fit into one of these groups: jocks, preppies, gang-bangers, heavy metal, mods, rockabillies or punkers.

Choosing punk rock came as naturally to me as eating. Everything about punk rock expressed who I had become at sixteen: aggressive, rebellious, violent, wild and hopelessly strung out. The beat and the lyrics for the most part, articulated the rebellion that had mushroomed within me. Identifying with the degenerate kids in punk rock took minimum effort on my part. We were kids lost in the shuffle. Our parents were too preoccupied elsewhere to pay attention. Their jobs and promotions on the corporate ladder meant little to us. Their shift from parents to pals confused us. Their divorces disillusioned us. Their pursuit of the American dream made us discontent. We answered with punk rock, the opposite of all that our parents stood for.

Void of restrictions and "the system" as we knew it, punk rock was an abusive, violent and wicked form of entertainment and expression. Slam dancing was a punker's interpretation of punk rock music. It was an adrenalin rush. This was not just "hardcore dancing." We actually tried to cut and hurt each other while we danced. Flying fists, jostling bodies, bloodied faces and hurling objects were not uncommon sights during the concerts where there was slam dancing. It was the perfect outlet for releasing years of my aggression and bottled-up anger!

Punk rock concerts were occasionally chaotic and violent affairs. There were nights when we went to a concert expecting a fun time only to end up in a clash with the police. The cops never hesitated to blast us with tear gas or clobber us with their billy clubs. Their aggressive and violent reactions to our concerts in their turf were equally returned when we harassed and pillaged the neighborhood. More than one of these uproars made the news.

One particular night, the Vandals[4] and some other old punk rock bands were doing a concert in a Los Angeles neighborhood. For whatever reason, one of my friends threw a beer bottle at the main sign of the building. The glass casing erupted into a million pieces and shattered on top of the police car below. A good excuse as any for the cops, they advanced with their billy clubs mercilessly beating the fleeing bodies. Tear gas was blasted everywhere. Momentarily we were trapped in a room filled with tear gas and maddened police with swinging vicious clubs.

But once we broke free from that room, our war cry was, "Let's fight!"

Chaos ensued. Adrenaline, anger, drugs and the frenzy drove our bodies and we wreaked havoc in that neighborhood. Kicking in the store windows, we destroyed what we could and looted the merchandise.

I turned at one point to see one my friends running down the street with a naked mannequin shouting, "Look what I got man!"

---

[4] An American rock band established in 1980 in Huntington Beach, California.

The accompanying violence did not deter me away from punk rock concerts. I loved the life I had chosen, even though I felt like I was looking for an elusive something. Still, drugs and punk rock were my escape. Close calls for my friends only shook me up for a while, but I soon learned to steel myself against those horrors. Such was the case when a punker friend was almost killed.

A Motorhead's[5] concert was a big deal especially when it was at the Olympic Auditorium. I was with a group of my friends at one of these concerts, and one of them was a crazy punker girl. Milling around with thousands of screaming people was a high in itself. But that day, our fun was cut short when someone stabbed the crazy punker girl with a screwdriver. The thrust had punctured her body.

We were all tripping out as we frantically bummed a ride to get her to the Los Angeles Hospital. As we were driving to the hospital still high on drugs we found ourselves laughing and freaking out at the same time because of the drugs. After the girl was admitted, we waited to hear news about her condition. There we stood high on drugs, looking all punked out, when in walked her parents. They took one look at us and dismissed us (not so nicely) as soon as they arrived.

With no ride and not knowing where to go, we decided to walk over to skid row with all the homeless people. That night on skid row, we hung out with the homeless and got drunk on Mad Dog 2020 and

---

[5] A British rock band formed in 1975 who "re-energized heavy metal in the late '70s and early '80s (www.wikipedia.org)."

Night Train. It only cost $1.00. We figured out how to buy cheap wine and get a good high.

Lowering the Bar

Lured by the punk lifestyle and music, drugs enhanced that experience. My mind was consumed with getting my next fix. Ordinary objects, like a spoon, triggered the desire to get more. Spoons were bent to put drugs or pills in to liquefy them. Then the liquid was shot into the arm for an insane high. Cotton from cigarette butts held the syringe back before administering the drug to the arm – all to the beat of punk rock.

Occasionally, I had reality checks. Once, in the stall of a filthy public restroom, as I drew toilet water into my needle, my mind screamed, "This is crazy. I'm sixteen and I'm shooting up out of a toilet." So fleeting was the thought! But it was enough to pester me later.

Punk rock was also about sex. The Sex Pistols band from England coined that. Punk rock started in a sex shop in London, England. Johnny Rotten, the lead vocalist of the Sex Pistols, started wearing bondage clothes and the kids in America ate it up. Time has done a facelift on punk rock though. It has mellowed out into a fashion statement for young people. Now punk rock is something cool and a subculture that MTV promotes. There is nothing wrong with that. However, it wasn't like that when I grew up.

Sex was a big part of my life. Hanging out at clubs and punk rock concerts and the world of drugs, exposed me to an excessive amount of lust and sex as a teenager. My mind began getting so perverted. In a matter of time, my friends and I were involved in the professional pornography business. This opened up opportunities for me to go to Mexico and also familiarized me with the sleazy parts of Hollywood. Waking up in a strange house in Mexico and having to find my friends to get back to the United States was no shocker. I was a kid and a prostitute, and I did not discriminate who I was with whenever the opportunity presented. AIDS was the big scare, but not for me. Nothing mattered because I was always loaded and had lost all commonsense.

Being a one-girl kind of guy was a joke to me. Cheating was a normal part of my life. I had been so exposed to perversion that if the opportunity to have sex presented itself, I took it. Since I hooked up with girls that were just as promiscuous as I was, they cheated on me as well. My conscience was seared on so many levels. Consequently when I got one girlfriend pregnant, it was no moral dilemma for me to accompany her to an abortion clinic. Even when Christians picketing at the clinic told us that abortion was murder, I simply turned a deaf ear to them. Later, the trip itself to the clinic proved a bother so that the next girl I got pregnant, I just gave her the money to get an abortion.

Abortions for my girlfriends were not the only horrible consequences of my sexually promiscuous life. I caught a bad venereal disease. That zapped the fun out of my sexual escapades. It also began to unravel whatever "fun" existed in my world. Also, encouraging my girlfriends to abort their pregnancies affected me later when I got married and wanted to have more children. What would life be like if I had those two other kids?

Tugs from the Hook

"This is religion. There's a liar on the altar..." sang John of the PiL (Public Image) punker band. Holding a circular fluorescent light over his head while mocking Jesus, John blasphemed God, prayer and the Bible. It was an overt appeal to denounce God and Christianity. Like everyone else in the audience at the Olympic Auditorium, I was eating up this music. Swept along by this frenzy, and spurred by a desire to belong to this crowd, I shouted and screamed in agreement with the singer. But the memory of that prayer I prayed at twelve-years-old kept cropping up.

Embedded in me were these haunting truths: God is real, heaven and hell are actual places, and the rapture will happen. No matter how low I went, they followed. It was remarkable that one prayer that I said years ago would not get out of my mind. Yet everything about me was anti-God. My selection of T-shirts displayed rebellion, hatred or the occult. Adolf Hitler was sported on one shirt while another had a pentagram with a goat's head in it. The music that I listened to was all anti-Christianity. Bands like Suicidal Tendencies, the Crass, Bad Religion, to name a few, were my main staple. I ran from God but I could not shake him. Even when tripping on acid, the truth would kick me in the back of the head. Like the time my friend claimed he was the antichrist who was going to give us the "mark of the beast" (666). Though we were all high on LSD, I knew he was wrong. The unforgettable altar call years earlier had basically inoculated me against such outrageous claims.

Occasionally, these harassing thoughts were pulled to the surface. That happened one time in continuation school. Alan, Ronnie and I were at my mom's house, and she was not home. My own apartment was just down the street. Our fix of angel dust and LSD (acid) took us on a wild ride. Hallucinations were expected when far out into the ethereal world of narcotics. But this bad acid trip was harrowing for Alan and Ronnie, and I heard it. Hell showed up in Alan's mind on my mom's front porch.

"Dude, I'm on fire!" Alan cried out.

"Man, I'm seeing like a lake of fire!" burst out Ronnie

Hearing them describe scenes that I had heard about in church freaked me out. We had gone overboard with the drugs.

"Dude, we have to call your dad!" Alan begged.

Dad was the only one we knew who went to church and could possibly help us. Though it was the middle of the night and dad's house was thirty minutes away, we thumped our way down there. Utterly terrified at the experience, we wanted relief.

Once at dad's house, Alan began ripping off his bondage bracelets.

He mourned, "Man, I can't take this anymore!"

In desperation, we confided in my dad "Something's wrong! We took way too many drugs. Pray for us." He did. And so did the people who were there that night. Thirteen hours later, we came off that high. We vowed that we were going to serve God.

Returning to the continuation school the following week, we wanted to see if those prayers worked. Armed with chick tracts, we stood in the school hallways handing them out to students as they spilled in and out of the classes.

"Hey man, you need to read this stuff!" we encouraged the students.

Roaming the hallways, we distributed the tracts in our punker outfits, while smoking weed and cigarettes. What a sight we were! Our enthusiasm lasted one week. Giving out chick tracts did not help us. We were still partying and getting high.

"Aw, forget it, man" one of us said. "Let's go party!" That ended it.

On more than one occasion, I came across people who tried to witness to me about Jesus. There was a club in Hollywood that was a regular haunt for my friends and me. It was there that I saw crazy punk rock bands like the Angry Samoans and the Butt Hole Surfers. It was also there that I ran into radical Christianity for the first time in my life.

We arrived at the club as usual, expecting the time of our lives. But three crosses and Christians preaching about Jesus confronted us. One of the crosses had "Jesus" hanging on it. Nice visual but also a nice target for a beer bottle. Throwing beer bottles at Jesus, we laughed them off. But they were not deterred.

Two Christian women singled me out of all people as a witnessing target. Jesus, they said, loved me and cared for me. I told them that I did not want to hear that junk. They persisted.

These girls are not afraid of us! I thought.

We looked completely wicked. To escape, I quickly bought a ticket and disappeared into the club thinking I lost these girls. The nice Christian ladies also bought tickets and followed me inside. Their presence and witnessing in the club bugged me. Walking by me with happy smiles (I knew they were not on ecstasy), they said that Jesus loved me. Nothing I said made them mad. They ruined my night.

****

In Whose Eyes

The danger we face today is that we categorize sins. One sin is not worse than the other. For the one who lived a perfect life, he is just as bad. He is still a sinner and a wretch like the one who did drugs and lived a horrid life. Paul called himself the chief sinner but he was a religious zealot. We should refuse to categorize sin and know that they are all the same in God's eyes.

God had more mercy with the prostitutes than the religious leaders. The Lord never put down the sinners, only the religious zealots. He called them a brood of vipers and children of the devil. God put me in the right church with the people who understand that type of compassion.

****

CHAPTER FIVE

A Hand in the Fire

Matters of Death

The bedroom window was shut. Our only way out of the house was through the kitchen – but they were there. Breakfast smelled awfully good, even through the ski mask. But the coke dealer and his brother had not invited us to breakfast – we were unwelcome guests stuck in his bedroom. To be caught red-handed robbing him was unthinkable. It could be deadly.

Alan and I had not planned on him returning home so soon. I knew the dealer. Knowing what time he usually left for work in the morning, Alan and I had waited for him to leave. Then we snuck inside the dealer's house. We were in the middle of ransacking his bedroom when we heard him and his brother return. Who would have thought that they had just gone to the store?

"We are dead!" we said in whispered tones. "These dudes are men and we are just boys."

"Okay, we gotta get out of here!" we signaled to each other.

Timing our flight out of the house through the kitchen was critical. So we just waited for a chance. No sooner had the men sat down to eat than Alan and I ran past them toward the door as our hearts pounded against our chests. Shocked, they grabbed at the door but Alan had reached it first and flung it open for me. One of them reached for my shirt and missed it by a mere inch. Alan flew one direction and I the other, each with a brother in hot pursuit. We got away.

Two months later, I went back to this drug dealer's house to buy drugs. He began to tell me the story of two guys who robbed his house. He had no idea who the culprits were because the ski masks had hidden their faces.

"Dang, dude, that is jacked up!" was my only response.

Obviously I was not scared enough to quit. Sometime later, I robbed from another dealer — just around the corner from me. His secret stash of coke was kept in the trunk of his Trans Am parked in front of his house was his secret stash of coke. He figured that if the cops ever searched his home, they would miss the stash in his car.

Once I got wind of the new coke supply in the Trans Am from his brother-in-law, I schemed to get it. The brother-in-law made a copy of the car keys. We intended to get that coke. Our chance to move in on the drugs came when the dealer went to a party and left the brother-in-law to baby-sit his kids. With our copy of the stolen car keys, we opened up the Trans Am trunk and feasted our eyes on a huge softball of pure coke. Jackpot!

But we were interrupted when cars pulled up to the house as we turned to leave. The dealer had just arrived with his friends. They saw us. Unsure whether they had seen what we had in our hands or not, we panicked at first and threw the coke on the ground. Then we picked it up and stuffed it in our clothes.

Moments later, the brother-in-law, a friend and me were huddled in the dealer's bathroom, with the lights dimmed, while we were shooting up. Outside the bathroom door, the dealer and his friends were pounding on the door. They were ticked off and enraged after finding their coke gone. Their rage, screaming and death threats fell on deaf ears.

"I'm going to kill you!" the dealer threatened his brother-in-law from the other side of the door, "I don't believe it's you."

"Listen, punk, you're going to die anyway," we told the guilty relative, "we can kill you right now or you can let those guys kill you later." We were sorry comforters.

"But that is your brother in law," I later reasoned, "I don't think he'll kill you."

We lost track of time. Then it happened again... another brush with death. My spoon sunk into the coke and I fell into blackness. The other guys saw me foaming at the mouth and vomiting through my nose. Dragging me to the backroom, they abandoned me there while they returned to the coke. I teetered between life and death. Coming to later in the back room, I only asked for my share of the spoil.

The fast track to hell had a hold on me that I could not loosen on my own. I was finding myself in a stronger bondage than I dreamed of. Nor could I stop my quick downward descent. And the close calls kept knocking.

Some friends and I were driving somewhere. We had all taken plenty of ROBO (a homemade drug made out of cough syrup) and as usual, I took the most. Suddenly, I began to freak out in my own urine. Just then, the cops pulled us over and asked me to put my hands on the hood of the cop car. I was so high from the drugs that I could not even see the hood. Reaching for it, I ended up putting my hands on the floor. How the cops got to believe my girl-friend's story about me being ill and how she was taking me to her house around the corner and calling an ambulance was beyond me. The cops should have taken me to jail. Panicking, my friends did call the ambulance, but when it showed up, I was coherent enough to refuse to get in it. My girlfriend at the time had seen enough and wanted no part of it…so she left me.

Deeper questions about eternity surfaced now and again like at the early death of Jimmie, one of my close friends. His death was a difficult blow to my crazy out-of-control life. He was one of my friends who took me to my first punk rock concert. Jimmie was riding in the backseat of an old car (with its engine in the back) with his girlfriend on their way to an LSD party, when their car was rear-ended and it exploded into flames. They never made it. Both were engulfed in the flames and died instantly. We heard the terrible news later from Jimmie's sister – all twenty-five or so of us at the party. Jimmie and his girlfriend were suddenly gone forever. I remembered thinking, *Where did they go?*

By the time I was seventeen, I had spent two years frequenting the coastal roads between California and Mexico for punker parties. Visiting cantinas and hanging out with my friends who surfed there were such a thrill. Those drives became more dangerous as my blackouts became more frequent. Awakening to find myself sleeping in front of my house with the car engine running, without having any idea how I got there, was one thing. Blacking out on a coastal cliff was quite sobering.

Once a girlfriend and I were driving back from Mexico and I was drunk. Though she was worried about me behind the wheel, I was belligerent about her not driving. With tequila in one hand and the steering wheel in the other, I zigzagged through the coastal land lined with cliffs. Then I blacked out and came to…right at the end of the cliff. My girlfriend became hysterical. Her crying, hitting and screaming at me for almost killing her was almost drowned out by my own wonderings…

What would have happened if I had died?

What if heaven and hell were real?

Close encounters with death were no deterrence from my destructive lifestyle. My first legal car was a 1972 Volkswagen bus when I was eighteen. It was demolished shortly afterward. Completely loaded, I drove through a red light and got sideswiped. The car rolled over and I shot out through the windshield. I walked away from that scene just a little banged up and cut, but alive.

Then I got a 1973 Volkswagen bus. It went the way of the first vehicle. Looking eagerly for a liquor store, a girl and I were busy scanning the opposite sides of the street, so neither of us was paying attention to the road, until it was too late. Two cars smashed into us. I rear-ended the car in front of me going 40 miles per hour, tossing the girl to the back seat. The Volkswagen bus was crushed into a Volkswagen. But I was not hurt.

Hardened. That was my heart. Evil had such a grip on me that I did not care, for I was willing to kill and hurt others...especially when feeling provoked.

It was a restless night and sleep eluded me. I hung around crazy people who did crazy things. That night one of the guys I knew came and urinated on my door. To let him get away with it was unthinkable. Moments later, I was outside beating the tar out of the guy. But he came back with his big brother...his big brother who looked like a mountain and I looked like an ant. Being skinny and dying from drugs, the advantage was on their side. My friend and I ran.

For two weeks, the big brother and his buddies harassed my friend and I. He chased us everywhere morning and night, making threats. The chase was becoming tiresome and our anger gave way to dark thoughts. What would it take to end it? Then I got it...

"Let's go make some Molotov cocktails[6]." I suggested.

Having filled a few beer bottles with gasoline and rags, we waited on the front porch of my house. The big brother arrived with his lot in a Volkswagen and parked. Armed with bats, two of them advanced toward us swinging them and ready to beat us.

I nudged my friend and said, "Dude, light that thing!"

Who cared if they lived or died? That was my mentality then. My friend hesitated. But I didn't. Lighting the bottles, I passed them to him.

"What am I supposed to do?" he asked nervously.

"Kill these dudes man!"

He looked scared.

"Do it, man!"

Pressured, he let a bottle fly toward the car. Whoosh! Gas splashed inside the vehicle and coughing guys spilled out of the car. The flaming rag fell out about four feet from the car, but it did not explode, thankfully. Their death or serious injuries would have been my doing.

Close to Home

By seventeen years old, the drugs had done their dirty work – I was shaky. Mom's diet pills disappeared into my system whenever I was at her house.

---

[6] A crude bomb made from a glass bottle filled with flammable liquid with a rag soaked in flammable liquid. The rag is then lit and the bottle is thrown at a target.

She was either oblivious to my addiction or was in complete denial of how bad it had become.

Endangering mom's life never occurred to me until I crossed Steven (not his real name). He was one of my junkie friends. Arms riddled with needle marks, Steven's veins were collapsing from drug abuse, but his desire to get a fix drove him to do anything – a passion that earned him an evil reputation. Beating up and robbing innocent people were things he did without flinching, and that made him a terror to the neighborhood. Tormenting him when he wanted food, for instance, was just for laughs (at least for me). Coaxing him to do crazy stunts like light his hair on fire for an unopened can of beans seemed funny. For the can opener, he had to relight his hair again. What I did not count on was Steven keeping score.

Offending Steven almost cost my mom's life. A group of my friends and I were partying and we took peyote cream. Steven was with us and as usual, he was no fun to be around. Ditch the dead weight was the group consensus. This obvious rejection angered Steven and he threatened to kill my mom. Extremely wasted from the drug, we just blew off his threat.

We partied hard that night until we were high out of our minds. Then, bunched up in the car, my friends and I drove past my house. As always, we all casually glanced over there. That is when we witnessed Steven climbing over the fence into my backyard. Mom was home alone. Feeling rather helpless because we were so wasted (I could not even talk), we kept on driving. Fortunately, the only sober friend in our group that night had the sense to call the cops because he was worried about my mom.

Steven was breaking into my house when the cops arrived. Unaware of being in any danger from Steven, mom asked the cops to let him go. He had pretended to be looking for me. And he somehow managed to toss the syringes he carried under the cops' car when they nabbed him. Mom did not know how close Steven came to making good on his threat that night.

Early the next morning, Shane escorted Steven over to my house on the handlebars of his bike. Though my head was still in a fog from the previous night's high, I read Shane's look of "This is your problem not mine." Depositing Steven on the front porch, Alan joined my other friends while I talked to Steven. My head was spinning lies to get rid of him. The best I came up with was to tell him that my mom was home and he had to leave. As he chewed on that, my friends and I melted out the back door then scaled the alley fence, abandoning Steven on my front porch.

He was not fooled. Still determined to get into my house, he crawled in through my window but was caught hiding in my closet by the police. That apparent break-in landed Steven in jail for a year. He pinned the blame on me.

A year later, I found out that Steven still carried a grudge. I was eighteen years old and very committed to selling LSD. Punk rock concerts were lucrative for selling dope and the Subhuman's (a hardcore punk rock band) concert at the Olympic Auditorium provided the opportunity. Never missing a chance to make a profit, I was there ready with my goods. People knew that I pushed acid. While making my rounds, I saw him. Steven was no more than five feet from me and he was with a group of skinhead punkers.

"I know he's here" I overheard him say. "I'm going to get him."

Instantly, I knew that he was talking about me. It was time to get away.

Physical changes to my appearance were my cover that day. Now a full-blown junkie with a skinny and weak body to prove it, my different punker look did the rest of the job. Steven did not recognize me.

"Kelly! Kelly!" shouted a girl wanting to buy drugs.

Steven's group turned around and looked at me but my feet kept moving. The girl continued to call.

"Kelly! Kelly!" I pretended not to hear her.

By then she was running to catch up.

"Kelly Lohrke!" She finally hollered out my full name in exasperation.

I turned and shushed her through gritted teeth, "You need to keep your mouth shut!" I was flipping out. Nervously I completed that sale and fled.

I skipped the concert that night and chose to stay in my car getting loaded all night until my brains were fried. Visited by a most wicked and tormenting experience, I could only cry out, "God, don't let me die tonight! Don't let me die tonight!"

My visit to my mom a month later confirmed my fears, Steven had a grudge and wanted revenge.

She was crying and obviously very upset about something.

"What's wrong?" I asked.

She explained, "That guy Steven came by. I just cracked the door open and he stuck a knife in the door and tried to force his way into the house."

He had then continued to threaten her through the door. It was time for mom to move.

Strange Bends

Then I met a girl named Sara (not her real name). We moved into a house together, with a coke and heroin addict friend named Dave as our roommate. Sara became my live-in girlfriend for about two years. Merely a front, neither of us was exclusively for the other – we both played the field and slept around. Sara and I both sold acid and hung out with friends in the pornography business. Our lives were perverted and uncontrollable.

But I wanted to stop – at least that morning. Barely able to control my shaking body, my mind was downloading hallucinations that curled up my insides. Hugging the porcelain was getting old. Even the eight ball ounce of coke at the party the night before did not appear so good then. Moderation was never my thing.

Like a madman, I was moaning to Sara, "I can't do this anymore. I've got to stop. I got to serve God. There has to be a God. I've got to stop all this madness."

Sara was sarcastic, "You're going crazy." (I really believed her.)

Watching me lay there on the bed in misery was frustrating for her. She knew the pull for a high was strong.

Finally she gave me an ultimatum "You know what, if you do coke again, I'm done," she said. "I'm leaving you, it's over!"

Not wanting to lose her quite yet, I promised, "No, I won't do it. I'm not doing that drug anymore."

A few hours later, there was a knock on my bedroom window. Peering out, I saw some of my friends holding up a bag of coke "Come on, man," they coaxed. "We've got a whole bunch."

Sara was draped on the bed listening to this exchange. She looked at me and warned, "If you do this, I'm leaving you."

Never batting an eye, I told her, "Get out of here! I'm done with you." Then I went out with my friends and got loaded. The pull inside me to get high was uncontrollable.

Sara and I split. She moved out of the house we rented because she said we could not afford it. With nowhere to go, I decided to go back to my mom's place. Her new condo apartment was a sign of her desire to start her life over. Gone was her old house, sold along with all the terrible memories. Mom initially refused to let me move back in with her. But then she agreed to let me stay for a week. I slept on her floor.

Life was coming at me fast, and I wanted off the train of self-destruction. Stopping it was something beyond my ability. On the morning the space shuttle Challenger exploded, hearing the tragedy on the television jolted me back to some reality. I told my mom that I wanted to be free. I was weary of abusing my body and enduring torments in my mind. Flushing the acid down the toilet that morning, I thought I was done. But the craving ran deep. Hours later, I was back selling and using acid.

Mom decided to get spiritual help for me – from a fortuneteller. She paid the psychic to read my future (not something I recommend). It was strange. The woman revealed that a female relative of mine was going to help me. Also that I was going to speak in front of a lot of people and that I was going to be famous. I was a loser then that was messed up. Somewhere in the recesses of my mind, I knew that God had His hand on my life. That prompted me to ask her whether she saw God in my future.

Reluctantly, she replied, "Religion is there if you want it. But that is what I see."

Two days later, my stepsister called.

"I heard you don't have a place to stay," she said. "Why don't you come and stay with me in Whittier?" This was just plain weird, especially that a psychic had said that a woman relative of mine was going to help me (I'm not endorsing psychics here).

My little apartment in Whittier was in the same complex as my stepsister's. Having my own apartment felt good. But my evil tendencies followed me there. Drugs, girls, and punk rock were my world. With my twisted mind, I faked a few car accidents so I could sue someone for money. (Later on, several cars were stolen from me and I wondered – coincidence or reaping what I had sown?). My life disgusted my sister.

I was a slave to my sex drive. Flirting with girls and women, I got them to sleep with me and then dumped them. Age mattered little because I made no distinction between mothers and their daughters (or if they were eight or eighty). One woman I slept with had a sixteen-year old daughter named Tracy (not her real name), who was as promiscuous as I was. Running into Tracy on my way back from the swimming pool was the beginning of a rocky and crazy relationship. Tracy would sneak over to my apartment to sleep with me. At nineteen, I had no desire to settle down so I still brought home other girls and that flipped out Tracy. She never understood that I liked her as a friend although I took full advantage of her infatuation with me. This relationship proved to be a snare to me later on.

CHAPTER SIX

The Last Straw

Dad's Shop

The machine shop was perfect. My boss and I both had the same side job — selling coke, meth and speed out of there. But that was a short ride. Catching one of the company owners cheating on his wife ended it. I caught him with his secretary at a hotel. With my big mouth, I broadcasted the affair. A few days later, the owner pulled me aside at another warehouse across the street. He was blunt. He was enraged. He was vengeful.

Threatening to cut off my private parts, he said, "You're dead, you little junkie! You just ruined my marriage." This was not an idle threat. Hit men came after me. It was time to drop out of sight.

Not knowing where to go, I called my father.

"Dad, I know that you haven't heard from me in a long time." I sounded awkward but it was the only logical choice. "Can I come work with you? I've got to get away. I'm losing my mind and there are some guys here that want to kill me. I need a place to hide out. Maybe I can live in grandpa's garage."

One of my grandpas had a house in Huntington Park in the Southeast area of Los Angeles. The house was rented out but the garage apartment was available.

Dad was kind. "Son, just leave and come here," he said.

So I did.

Lohrke's Forklift Place resembled a junkyard – dusty, filthy, and littered with old cars and car parts. Dad never threw anything away. His forty-some-year-old business was an eyesore for the city. But business had been good. Cleaning up around the shop and picking up parts for $6 an hour was easy enough. Drugs had fried my brains so that I was not good for much. So I gave up my San Francisco LSD connection to one of my friends. This was the beginning of 1987.

Working for my dad was uncomfortable. He was a Christian, but a half-hearted one. All the employees had to wear a uniform with two patches on it. One read "In God We Trust" and the other said, "Jesus." As much as I hated it, wearing the uniform saved my clothes from dirt and grease.

Prayer was mandatory before work each day. Everyone complied. Dad had the strength of an ox and looked intimidating in his over-six-foot frame. Standing in a circle holding hands, each person had to pray. Being a heathen was not an exemption. Nor was being loaded an excuse.

"Jesus, help us today," I slurred, while my mind cried out, "Jesus, just don't kill me now." I was convicted and condemned at the same time. Unable to stomach this insanity, I decided to come to work late – to make sure I missed the prayer meeting.

Walking into work an hour late, loaded and quite pleased with myself, I heard my dad announce to everyone, "Okay guys, Kelly's here, let's pray!"

This continued day after day and it did not matter whether I was late thirty minutes or an hour, dad waited to include me. That messed with my head.

Then the cover came off one night – for my dad. My friends and I had just left a concert. A parked car in the street looked awfully familiar. Being loaded did not hamper our ability to recognize someone in there that we all knew.

"Dude, isn't that your dad's car?" asked one of my friends.

"Yeah," I admitted. Dad's features were distinguishable enough from the distance.

We drove closer we drove until we pulled up and saw dad with a prostitute.

I looked at him and sneered, "Hey, Christian! See you tomorrow at work!" And then I added, "Don't you ever tell me about that Jesus again." Then we drove off.

How I looked forward to work the next day! I was going to rail on my dad for being a hypocrite. But something else happened...

As I approached him ready to tell him off, Dad just broke down and cried. Then he began to tell me his story about the abuse he went through as a child. Oh, how he wanted to be free from the torment! At the time, Dad struggled with lust (something he later admitted to me), but he did not see it then. The way dad talked baffled me. Him openly admitting his pain was disturbing. It was hard to hear my dad share his past, one that included being sexually abused by a leader in a church as a child. The abuse led him to deal with feelings of rejection, sexual addiction and deep-rooted bondages. To see my dad, such a big strong man cry and looking so weak at that moment, really tore me up inside. I did not know what to do with what I was feeling. Anguish was growing within me...

Life in the Garage

Alone in my garage apartment, my soul was vexed. Life seemed to have me in a stranglehold. Dad's vulnerable moment and confession bugged me. And worst of all were the tormenting dreams. The theme was the same — the lake of fire, missing the rapture and getting my head chopped off. Waking up in fear, I vowed to quit, flushed my drugs down the toilet and went on my way. Just for a day.

But my mind, warped by drugs, yelled, "What in the world did you just do?"

Back I went to get my fix. The dreams kept coming. And this insanity and emotional roller coaster continued for three weeks. Was I going crazy? Was I losing my mind?

A few yards away from me, in my grandpa's house, a family was praying for me. Striding up their driveway about a month ago, I had rocked their world. I was a punker, and they were not.

Eyeing me through the window, the Menchaca family sighed inwardly, "Oh my God! What did we do?"

They had agreed to let me stay in the garage apartment as a favor to their landlord – my grandpa. That was before they saw me. I looked and acted like everything they did not want their children to be. Now it was too late to change their minds.

So they began to pray, "God, please either save this boy or make him move."

As they prayed, I found the bottom of the pit.

Living about four weeks in the garage in mental torture was hellish. I felt so torn up inside. Even the three-day crystal meth binge where sleep escaped me only pushed me closer to the edge. On the third day, I drove down to Long Beach to meet my friends at a punk rock concert.

Being in full form as a punk rocker attracted attention. People on the highway stared. Was it curiosity, amusement or pity? Whichever it was, their stares only irked me. It made all that I was living with want to be unleashed on them. Finally, I lost it when some guys in a nearby car laughed at my punker hair.

"Forget these dudes!" I raged and drove off the freeway, over the embankment and rolled the car in the process. But it righted itself and I kept on driving.

Rage had me in a headlock and it felt like a beast was taking over me.

The several fights I got into that night did not satisfy the rage and bully inside me. My friends and I ended up at a girl's house that night. We violated her. Then a wicked desire to kidnap and rape someone grew. I yielded to it in the middle of the night.

Driving from Huntington Beach to Pacific Highway, I combed the streets for a prey. Like a starving shark, I wanted to find someone to exploit.

Anyone.

Yet, the sunlight found me driving around with no prize. There had been no prey. No one to kidnap and rape – and the speed was wearing off. A deep depression accompanied by a dark emptiness was creeping in. Nothing could hide me from the dreadful feeling. The long night had ended and it was eight o'clock on Saturday morning.

I parked my car in front of the house. Albert always watched me come up the driveway from his front window. I never minded that before. But that morning, my desire to be invisible from his family's eye was strong. Yet, it was not comparable to the rising hatred inside me for the way I lived and felt. Squatting down on the driveway, I slinked into the garage.

Then the unexplainable happened.

My deep longing came…

Barely stepping into the garage apartment, I fell on my knees and wept uncontrollably. It hit me. I was done. It was time. I wanted freedom from my wicked life so bad. It was something like I have never felt before. I needed change!

Between sobs, I cried out to Jesus, "God, if you are there, please touch me! Jesus, Jesus, if you are real, like the neighbors are telling me about, come into my heart. Everyone else seems to bother me about you. And you are gonna have to do a miracle in my life. I don't want to die. I'm so tired. Please come into my heart, I surrender."

And I cried for two hours until I could cry no more. It felt like Jesus was cleaning me out of all the wickedness inside of my life. Something was happening inside me that I had never experienced and there was no high that ever made me feel like I did at that moment. Then, I got up — completely changed, forever.

Straightening up the best I could, I ventured out to Albert's front door and knocked. He opened the door and saw me standing there with eyes like tomatoes.

"I think I just got saved," I kept repeating. "I think I just got saved."

He looked at me and slowly smiled.

That was February of 1987.

That Was My Life

Why write this book? Was it to boast about my past life or glorify the debauchery of sin? Never. God challenged me about sharing my testimony.

I was coming up to my 20-year anniversary of being a believer when I felt the Lord compel me to share the detailed accounts of my past. These were details I had never shared before.

The Lord led me to read and study Matthew 1 — the genealogy of Jesus Christ. His lineage was peppered with some interesting characters. There was Abraham who lied about his wife being his sister to save his own skin (two different times!); Jacob the deceiver; Rahab the prostitute; Judah guilty of incest (slept with his daughter-in-law because he thought she was a prostitute); and King David, an adulterer, liar and murderer. All these people were messed up in some way and blew it big time. Right smack at the beginning of the New Testament, Jesus' descendants were listed as if He was saying that He was not at all ashamed of them.

The point is this – God was merciful when he reached down and rescued my life from depravity. My life was dark and deep in sin. I understand to some extent what Paul the apostle said when he called himself the "chief sinner." I certainly lived a life of one who was so lost. My life reminded me also of Newton's, the man who wrote the song "Amazing Grace." He was a wretched man, an evil slave trader, and one that destroyed lives, but God saved him.

The intent and purpose of this book needs to be clear. Out of darkness, God can bring something good. This testimony is meant to inspire. I know some of these stories are hard to read and graphic in details. Some people might ask, "Where is he going with this?" or "What is the purpose?" If you are a Christian and think that way, consider this: the first portion of this book is geared to reach the lost. But I challenge you to read on.

The first section is mostly to challenge a Christian not to neglect the worst of society. You never know what God can do in someone's life. Even when you meet, see or witness to people for the first time, you don't know the pain they may have lived through. Sure you might see the pain on their faces, but the details of that pain are hidden from you. God might want to make trophies out of them.

To the unbeliever or backslider who reads this book, God is the God of grace, mercy and second chances. God can change you. Haven't you had enough?

"For we have spent enough of our past lifetime in doing the will of the Gentiles — when we walked in lewdness, lusts, drunkenness, revelries, drinking parties and abominable idolatries. In regard to these, they think it strange that you do not run with them in the same flood of dissipation, speaking evil of you (1 Peter 4:3, 4)."

PART TWO

BUILD ONE: THE DISCIPLE

CHAPTER ONE

Unhooking from the Fury

A Whole New World

Still dressed in my punk rocker gear – blue hair, knee-high boots and leather jacket, I followed Albert and Yolanda to the church. No need to wear a suit to church, they had said, it was "come as you are." But I stood out like a sore thumb. Not only was I the only white guy (besides the pastor), I was the only punk rocker. Hundreds of people from this rough neighborhood were drawn to this church, including mostly Mexican gang-bangers! Feeling intimidated was putting it mildly – I was afraid. Gang-bangers were the kind of people who either bought drugs from me or chased me.

Oh, I'm dead! I thought. *These guys kill guys like me.*

If Albert and Yolanda were still leery of me, it was understandable. After all, it was only yesterday that I was in a murderous spirit. My speech was slurred and I spoke with great difficulty (thanks to all the drugs). It would take time to assure them that I had "died" to who I was on the floor of the garage yesterday.

Albert kindly introduced me to the guy at the door.

"Hey, Steve, this is Kelly. He just got saved yesterday."

This was Sunday evening. Though Albert and Yolanda had invited me to the Sunday-morning service, I slept right through it. Pure exhaustion had me dead to the world from the night before until Sunday afternoon.

But all my fears left when the worship began. Hands all around that place lifted to heaven in surrender – tattoos and all. In my heart, I knew I was home. These gang-bangers were Christians. They may look like gang-bangers but they were changed people.

A man named Pastor Jimmy Joe Lewis was preaching that night. He talked fast and fervent. When he gave the altar call for anyone who needed God in their life, I practically ran up there. I needed God badly. Albert followed to pray with me. That was my public surrender to Jesus.

Finally I was free. Nothing could persuade me otherwise that night. Since yesterday when I had prayed in the garage, all my cravings for drugs, ciga-rettes or even alcohol had evaporated! I also had zero withdrawals. This was purely supernatural. From the time I was fourteen years old until yesterday, I could not remember a day when I was sober. Now being sober was the new high.

"What do you think of the church?" Albert's voice cut into my thoughts.

Without hesitating I sputtered enthusiastically, "It is my new home. I'll never leave that place." I really meant it.

Come Monday, I saw that I had a visitor when I drove up to the garage. Parked in my driveway was an old blue Mustang driven by a guy that looked like a gang member. He had a card in his hand and it was obvious that he was waiting for me. Albert was not even home.

"I saw you at church Sunday," he began. "I wanted to see how you are doing."

I was a little freaked out.

"Can I come in?" he asked.

"Sure."

For thirty minutes, he stayed and visited and then he prayed for me before he left. Every day that week, this guy came by just to visit. That blew me away. Such a concept may freak out people now (especially if we have been saved for some time), but as a new convert, those daily visits were what I needed. I was a new baby Christian and did not need to be left alone. Forever I will be grateful for those who invested their lives in mine in those early years as a Christian, like that man.

****

Hold the Snake Oil

The Holy Spirit had drawn me to that church. That service reminded me of the powerful church meeting in Acts 2:40 when the Holy Spirit fell on the people. Peter preached and multitudes from all walks of life were saved. He called the people to come and "be saved from this perverse generation." I saw myself as one of those "perverse" people, a sinner.

Unfortunately, it is not popular to deal with the issue of sin in this generation anymore. Peter had no fear telling the truth. He told his audience to repent and they "gladly received the word and were baptized." Now churches are selling the world a snake oil, which is a form of godliness that denies the power of God. The power of God changed me so that I was instantly delivered from years of addictions, and a destructive lifestyle. Plus, I experienced no withdrawals.

But that was not the end of it. The rest of that story said that the believers continued "steadfastly in the apostles' doctrines." Their fellowship was not just for fun (although that was part of it). Neither was their emphasis on church growth. Their concern was more about getting together to learn the truth of the gospel – true doctrine, and to grow as Christians.

We need to abandon our fears of preaching biblical repentance. Our emphasis also needs to shift from church growth to Christian growth. For when we do, we will see the power of God begin to change lives in dramatic ways that are purely supernatural.

****

Burning My Bridges

I fled the garage at three in the morning. Standing distressed and naked in front of Albert's door, I was pounding desperately.

"Albert, help me!" I cried.

My kind neighbor opened the door, assessed the situation in mere seconds and let me his house.

"Come in."

Albert and his wife covered me. Still trembling from fear, I began to tell them the reason for my intrusion at three o'clock in the morning. A demonic being was sitting on my stomach, choking me as it tried to enter my body. That woke me up.

"Jesus!" my voice pierced into the night.

The evil thing jumped off me. I bolted out of the garage and headed to the neighbor's house.

"Albert, I'm scared," I cried. "I'm still a punker! I'm still dirty!" My conversion had been but a few weeks. Though I was completely free from my past addictions, the demonic harassments were still happening.

"Stay with us," Albert offered.

As filthy as I felt, Albert and Yolanda prayed for me and then let me crash on their couch. (Later, Albert told me that he felt the spirit of fear when I entered his home.)

This phenomenon was not new. Occasionally, this type of demonic visitation happened to me as a boy when I stayed at my father's house. Dad was the one who dragged me to church as a child. But generally, the scenario was the same – something evil would jump on me and wake me up. Paralyzed from fear, I would lay there while my body felt like it was on fire.

Once while staying with my aunt and uncle, the demon woke me up and my cousin witnessed me frozen with fear. He called my aunt and uncle for help. That only raised my aunt and uncle's suspicion that I was causing trouble. They sent me back home. Interestingly enough, these harassments never happened at my mom's.

Much later, I led my younger cousin to the Lord. He was in a punk rock band and made a decision to serve God. That night as he slept on the couch, a demon jumped on him causing his body to be on fire (could it have been the same one?). He looked spooked as he told me about it in the morning. Strangely enough, another friend of mine named James Kelton stayed at my home and had vouched for the same torment. I linked the harassments to the old punk rock lifestyle I led and the doors I had opened in my life to the devil.

At the same time, my new life as a Christian was revolutionary. A brand-new baby Christian needs a good home church. Praise Chapel became that place for me. I was discovering the importance of being around God's people – especially for a new convert. They were my new family. What I had found was valid and wonderful, and I did not want to lose it. The more I heard God's Word preached and taught, the more I changed my life. A desire to be solely sold out to God grew. My old life had no appeal to me. I took Jesus' words to heart when He said that if your right arm makes you sin, cut it off (Matthew 5:30). And it's better to go to heaven with one arm that to go to hell with two. Well, I wanted to get rid of every hindrance.

So I asked myself, "I don't want to go to hell. What is my right arm? What is it that makes me sin?"

Drugs were not it anymore.

Nor was it family.

Friends? Definitely.

Though a fairly new convert, I knew that my old friends were "bad company" for the new life I had chosen (1 Corinthians 15:33). Distancing myself from them was not too difficult because when I moved to the garage, few of them knew my phone number or where I lived. I developed new friendships with people from the church. Fellowship was such a part of the church that either I was at someone else's house or I had people over to my garage apartment. Soon, I discovered that there was another stumbling block in my life.

I was the new guy in church, the only white guy and a punker. Combined, those factors were enough to attract attention. People were also fascinated with my past. Whenever people from the church were over at my house, they asked to see my photo albums. These were filled with mementos of my past life: crazy pictures of my friends and me, a cigarette butt or unfinished joint attached here and there. Treasured collections of punk rock music and stuff from my previous lifestyle were strong reminders of my old love. Within me was an increasing desire to be free from any entanglements to my old life. I realized what I had to do. No one had to tell me. I knew what God was saying to me.

In the corner of my garage apartment was a little fireplace. With armloads of punker clothes, the jacket with the patches of the bands I'd seen, the spikes, boots, records and picture albums, I piled them near the fireplace. The whole stack represented my old identity, my past and what had filled my life – darkness, depression, destruction, hurt and pain. God was defining my life in a new way and I wanted that more than anything else.

Kneeling down on the garage floor, I prayed, "Jesus, this is my life. This is what I was. I don't like it. And I don't want anything to do with this anymore. I want to burn my bridges. I don't want to go back." Whatever it took to serve God, I was willing to do it. "Jesus here is my life. You can do whatever you want to do with it."

Then I fed the heap of stuff to the fire to the tune of Keith Green's song "I Make My Life a Prayer to You." I even broke my television set.

Swirling black smoke from the garage chimney and a stinky odor (plastic records are stinky when burnt) sent Albert rushing into the garage.

"What happened?"

There I was, seated amidst a pile of clothes, records, photo albums, and loose pictures, feeding them into a blazing fire (twenty years or so later, when I needed photos for a slideshow of my testimony, some old friends had to mail me photos for it).

"I don't want anymore of this stuff. I don't ever want to backslide" was my reply.

Then I pleaded with Albert. "I need you in my life. I need someone to teach me how to pray." At the time, I couldn't even read right.

Albert took me under his wing from that day on, and he began to teach me how to read and pray.

****

The Gathering Places

Meeting together with other believers is essential to the well-being of a believer. The New Testament church met together often and went from house to house breaking bread (Acts 2:46). Their differences did not keep them apart nor did it keep them from having all things in common. Possessions were things they held onto loosely. Jesus was the one who brought them together and the focal point of their gatherings. It was in one of those gatherings places where the Holy Spirit fell on them.

Fellowshipping with other believers was vital to my survival and growth as a new convert. God chose Praise Chapel as the place for me to be nurtured, grow and be trained in the things of God (1 Corinthian 12:18). Staying where God planted me resulted in my life beginning to flourish (Psalm 92:13-15). Good things happen when believers join together often to fellowship. We are promised that when we stay and flourish where God sets us, we will still bear fruit in our old age! Hanging out with God's people at Praise Chapel taught me faithfulness and loyalty – these are values to be treasured.

Unfortunately, we live in a generation of people who are easily offended and lack loyalty. We see this with parents, children and spouses and evident in the increasing number of broken homes. All spectrums of society including the church suffer from this trend. Finding loyal people is almost a rarity.

We have learned to be distrusting and to cut and run when offended. As a result we have people who never seem to reach their potential because they move from church to church without ever staying long enough in one place. Thus we have the "church hopping" phenomenon among Christians today. Growth in numbers for some churches has been due to fish transferring from other fish bowls to another instead of the churches reaching into the deep ocean. Meanwhile, the unchurched remains untouched. But in the New Testament church, there was no other church to pick from so people had to learn to get along.

Sadly, some of this shifting around is due to countless people being hurt and violated in church. The wound often seems deeper because we expect the church to be a safe place. But not all those who come to church have it all together or are safe people. Church is a good place to practice forgiveness, even when some there curse us (yes, of all places!). Never forget the words of Jesus about blessing those who curse us (Luke 6:28). I'm not condoning obvious abuse or sinful corruption, for with such acts, the perpetrators need to be dealt with and held account-able. The abuses and corruptions need to stop. My point is that we are a culture that gives up too easily on relationships.

Blessings are linked to places. In those places, the lives of the people there become entwined with ours. People don't join churches: God puts them there. Yet, God always has a plan at work when dealing with us while in those places. We do not always understand why God chooses the places he does, and yet He does. He always keeps the big picture in mind. Moving from a place due to offenses and bitterness may not kill us but we will miss something great in our lives. Hardships do come. But as Paul reminded Timothy, when the hardships come, he was to "endure" as a "good soldier." The same is required of us. He never meant for us to run away from them.

■■■

I Live Where I Sleep

Wadding up my leather jacket, I would say, "I live here tonight."

And for that night, I would stay there. Being late or never going home was normal. Hanging out with my friends was better than going home. Mom never knew my whereabouts for this was before cell phones and pagers. Whenever I felt like it, I would show up at home with hideous tattoos. Such was my life before I was saved.

Church became my life after I got saved. Surrendering my life to Jesus for me meant that I was at church all the time, whenever the church doors opened. Besides working a job, I spent time going to Bible study, outreaches, prayer meetings, drama practices or follow-ups. As a sinner, I sold out to the devil, and there was nothing lukewarm about my commitment. I was a fully committed punk rocker, drug addict and sinner. Now as a Christian, I became completely sold out to God. It was all the way for Jesus and nobody could change my mind.

My family certainly knew of my excitement about my newfound faith. Unfortunately, my new passion offended them.

"Why are you not here?" they would complain. "Why don't you ever visit?"

Mom began to wonder if I had joined a cult. My going to church in an area of town where she would not dare drive down to was part of her concern. Keith Green's song that he wrote to his family rang true with me. I had said goodbye to my family as a punk rocker. Now, I said goodbye to them again when I got saved.

Looking back, do I regret the way I was before? Yes. But if I had to go through the punk rock life to hit rock bottom and then become a Christian who lives a zealous and passionate life for God to make me the pastor I am today, I'd do it all over again. To be saved, I had to be lost first. And I was really lost.

■■■

Sold Out

Burnout is a not a concept that I see in the Bible. But I see lukewarm, "lukeout", and excuses called copouts. God calls us to live radically for him. Even excuses such as "I just got married" or "let me bury my father" or "I have to check out my new land" do not fly when it comes to responding to God. I think more Christians need to know how much they need to sell out to God.

The culture may have changed but Christians do not need to compromise and water down their commitments. Living radically for God is the only way. Otherwise, evaluate your life. How are you living now by just going to church sporadically? Are you satisfied with where you are spiritually? Maturing in your faith comes by much intake of God's word, worshipping, fellowshipping, witnessing, attending church and Christian ministry to the Lord.

Selling out to God is explained in Luke 14. Jesus said that if we don't sell out to God we could not be His disciples. Wow! Compared to our love for Christ, our love for everyone and everything else would be as hatred. These are strong, challenging words. There is a call in Luke 14:26 to "forsake all." We wrestle with such scriptures in our Christianity. For me, I had forsaken all once before (for punk rock) – now it was time to forsake again to go pray, fast and witness. Forsaking friends, family and a culture that was my lifestyle (punk rock), and even things I thought were right, was my answer to God's call. No doubt the flesh fights this, but we don't give up. We keep pressing in.

Here is the road to discipleship – complete abandonment to Jesus. God takes the clay of our lives, like the clay in the hand of a potter, and makes it to be something He can use. Our words alone are not enough. Talk is cheap.

Many are like the guy who offered to follow Jesus wherever He went (Luke 9:57). Jesus was calling him to be a disciple. But the guy did not say "no." He just wanted to be excused to first go and bury his father. The story does not even say that his dad was dead. This was an attitude of priority. Perhaps the guy's motivation was financial. So Jesus set it to him straight, and He told him to let the dead bury the dead. Ouch!

Someone else desired to follow Jesus but first wanted to say good-bye to his family. Jesus' response was that "no one after putting his hand to the plow and looking back is fit for the kingdom of God (Luke 9:62)." Ouch again! The time was right for both men to follow, but they were not quite ready to say goodbye to everything. Are you?

The Holy Spirit is calling daily for someone to bring glory to the Father. But some Christians are so hung up on "callings." There is one calling for a Christians – to go and preach the Gospel to every creature. That way we can be a blessing and show Jesus' compassion to the world.

****

Enter the Holy Spirit

Three weeks into salvation, Albert took me to another Bible study — this was after our Bible study. His brother, Rudy, and I began a conversation. Rudy knew that I was a new convert. He asked me how long I had been saved and I told him that it had been a few weeks.

"Have you been baptized with the Holy Spirit?" he queried. This was something new.

"What is the Holy Spirit?"

Rudy explained to me that being baptized with the Holy Spirit is a gift from God. "If God had a gift for you would you want it?"

"Sure."

Then he said, "Let's go in the back room and pray."

Everything that God said I could have, I wanted. I was ready. Lifting my hands upward, I asked for the baptism of the Holy Spirit. Instantly, a most unusual language came out of my mouth. It sounded so amazing and overwhelming that my eyes popped open. I felt like I was just hit by a truck. Sometime later, I came to fully understand what I had received that day.

Immediately, things began to happen that were totally new to me. Standing in line at the 7-Eleven with my Big Gulp soda the following Monday, I felt a new unction. Something in my chest and head said, "Tell them that I love them." There was no way I was going to yell out anything inside a 7-Eleven in Los

Angeles. They would think I was trying to hold up the store or rip them off.

I said, "No."

It kept building and building inside me, until I blurted out, "Excuse me, everyone, I want to tell you that Jesus loves you."

Then I put the soda down and ran out of there completely freaked out.

Yolanda was hanging clothes on the clothesline by the garage when I got home. My eyes must have told her that something had scared me. My heart was still racing.

Searching my face she asked, "What on earth happened?"

I said, "I think I did something wrong."

She was concerned. "What did you do?"

I told her.

"Oh Kelly, you got filled with the Holy Spirit," she said, "That is what the Holy Spirit is for, to make you preach the gospel."

Something radical was birthed inside me that day.

****

Dynamic Empowerment

Paul came across people like me. Twelve men. Apparently, these men were disciples who believed in Jesus Christ but had not received the baptism of the Holy Spirit (Acts 19:1-6). Actually, they had not even heard there was a Holy Spirit (verse 2). But they were open to receiving all that God had for them. When Paul laid hands on them, they spoke in tongues and prophesied.

It is possible that these men were believers for a while but had not received this gift. Paul recognized that they needed the baptism of the Holy Spirit. They needed the power of the Holy Spirit (or *dunamis* in Greek – where we get our word dynamo or dynamite) for service.

> *"But you shall receive power when the Holy Spirit comes upon you (Acts 1:8)."*

Baptism in the Holy Spirit is an explosive power available to every believer in Jesus Christ. Jesus asked his disciples to wait for this power of the Holy Spirit on the day of Pentecost. Evidently, they needed it to minister. God's gift of the Holy Spirit enabled them to serve God and bear fruit.

Today, the baptism of the Holy Spirit is a matter of doctrine only and not a demonstration of power. Some denominations feel superior because they speak in tongues. That is missing the point. Peter and the disciples after being baptized with the Holy Spirit went out and street preached. The gift was not just for the church. This is an empowerment for service. It is the boost we need to be witnesses for the gospel.

Paul did not condemn the twelve men because they had not been baptized in the Holy Spirit (Acts 19). He merely asked them if they wanted to receive this gift because they already believed. Verse 10 said they continued for ten years. A major shift occurred in the ministry when these twelve men received the Holy Spirit. Could it be the missing factor for many believers today?

****

Closing an Old Door

Waking up to demonic harassment was no way to start off a day. Increasingly, they were becoming frequent and menacing. Going home to the garage was now a dread. A fellowship of about twenty or thirty people from church was ending one night, and people were saying their goodbyes and heading out the door. But I just hung around -delaying the inevitable. Dennis, one of the guys there, saw me. He knew why I did not want to leave.

Pulling me aside, he asked, "Kelly, do you know that you have power in the name of Jesus to conquer the enemy?" No one had told me that yet. He advised, "You need to leave the door open and tell that demon to leave."

I asked, "Like Clint Eastwood when he said, 'Make my day!' and 'Do you feel lucky?'" Dennis nodded.

That did it. I went home angry that night – at the demon. Opening the garage door, and not bothering to turn on the lights, I announced to the demon that I was not afraid of it. Also, I told it that I was not returning to my old life. Then I told it to leave. Without missing a beat, I then went through every room of that garage and began to pray in tongues.

My prayer language from the Holy Spirit was my strength for that battle. The demonic harassments stopped.

God was delivering me from all the bondages that were associated with my old life. He had saved me, delivered me from drugs without withdrawals, healed me of the hepatitis and venereal disease (my wife had me checked for that last one before our wedding), and now I was set free from a major fear and torment. Yet another haunt from my past was about to enter my life.

The Decoy

Moving into the garage was life changing for me in many ways. The low profile I took helped. I cut loose most of my friends and only a few people knew my phone number. Sara, the sixteen-year old girl I had messed around with, was not one of them. But that did not stop her from seeking me out. Two months later, after I became a Christian, she came looking for me at my dad's shop. Dad witnessed to her and, out of the kindness of his heart, brought her to Praise Chapel.

I was naive as a new convert. Seeing an old friend get saved was exciting. We hung out together because we were friends. No one had told me at that point that it was not wise to be alone with a girl. Sara and I soon fell into sin. Every time I slept with her I was tormented but I did not know any better. Thankfully, I did not get her pregnant. Sara had fallen totally in love with me – feelings that I did not return. She began to express these feelings to me.

It was not long before one of the church leaders found out that I slept with Sara. His immediate solution was that I had to marry her. Jumping into bed with a girl was something that I had done before without caring. Now I was different. Doing the right thing was important to me. I truly loved the Lord and did not want to disobey Him in anyway and hinder the growth in my life. Still, I felt obligated to do it and scraped up some money to buy her a ring.

Albert, my mentor and teacher, definitely needed to know about my impending marriage to Sara, and so I told him. His "okay" was not an agreement with my decision but rather an "okay, if that is what you want to do" response. Albert was not a controlling person. Pressure to marry Sara was mounting from the church leader and his wife. And I went along with it…for a while.

My engagement to Sara was rocky and distracting. Picking her up from school was one of the things I did. Drugs were occasionally in her purse. Since God had removed the desire for drugs from my life, this was not a temptation at all. But I could not resist Sara. She would flirt with me and we would fall into sin. I did not want to do it but did it anyway. The torment was becoming unbearable, especially because I had made this commitment to go for God.

And the pressure from the one church leader and his wife kept building. They assured me that everything was going to get better after I married this girl. Praying about things was not something I had learned at this point. Knowing the will and destiny of God for my life were revelations I had not grasped yet. But something seemed wrong.

My uneasy feeling about the whole engagement grew with Sara's increasing tantrums. Once on our way to church, she threw a fit because she did not want to go.

"Take me home now!" she demanded, "I don't want to be here!"

Now I wanted to be in church. Retreating to the prayer room, I began to cry. A guy named Larry Garcia (now my brother-in-law) and another man named Jeff Johnson saw me crying and came up to me.

"What's the matter?" they asked.

Between sobs I said, "This stinking, stupid girl!" (That was the way I talked then.) "I don't want nothing to do with her! I have to marry her and I don't think it's fair that I gotta marry her. They told me it's God's will. I pick her up and she is loaded. We are messing up. I don't wanna live this way! I don't feel this."

Larry stated, "This is not God's will." Then he asked, "Who told you that?"

I told him.

"This is wrong." he cautioned, "Kelly, you don't need to marry her. It will mess up your life. Don't do this!"

"What do I do? I'm engaged to her. I got plans." I mourned, "Her grandparents know and my family knows."

"Don't do this! This is not God." Larry urged. His words set right with me.

"You're right, man," I admitted. "I don't want to do this, but how do I get out of it?" I had to find out for myself.

Sara was still engrossed in a fit that night and refused to talk. She just looked out the window and ignored me. When we got to her place, she slipped the ring off her finger and placed it on the console.

In my mind I thought, "Good!"

She was only seventeen and playing a little game.

I told her, "If you take that ring off, you are not getting it back."

She remained silent. With a slam of the jeep door behind her, she was gone in a huff. I pocketed the ring and felt such a peace from God like I've never felt before.

Breathing out a "Thank God!" I began to sing and worship the Lord. "In the name of Jesus, in the name of Jesus, I have the victory," my voice sang into the night. After two months of being severely distracted with Sara, I felt like I was saved all over again. For sure, I knew that the engagement was off.

Sara stayed around the church for a while even after we broke up. Though her feelings for me remained strong and she made attempts for a few months to get me back, I was done with the relationship. Not even her friends telling me that it was wrong made me change my mind. Besides, I had found a new passion – street preaching.

CHAPTER TWO

The Making of a Preacher

Taking It to the Streets

Right on the street corner where the church stood was a sort of "divine chaos." People in our church had taken the gospel to the streets, preaching and witnessing to others. Our pastor's response to this was "Go for it!" Young men were out there daily on a street corner of Los Angeles preaching the gospel and sharing their testimony using a bullhorn. They were not ashamed of their faith, nor were they intimidated in any way. I began to notice this while driving to church one evening. Apparently, this was a normal practice. Two hours before services, these men arrived early – one hour to preach and one hour to pray.

Brother George Verdugo was the loudest and boldest preacher out there. After watching him for a while, I decided, "I want to do this." They gave me the bullhorn and I began to tell my testimony.

No one told me I had to street preach. The desire came from watching other young men of God boldly do it. Street preaching was soon part of my regular routine. Every day after work, I went home, took a shower and then we went out and preached. People were getting saved on the corner and then went to church. But we weren't without our challenges. We were cussed and honked at, but we did not stop. In the process, we saw many people become radically saved. We were not wackos preaching condemnation (i.e., the end of the world or death to homosexuals), but we were preaching the saving power of God to a dying world.

Our lives felt purposeful. We felt that wherever we were, it was no accident. We took it to mean that we could witness to whoever was there, whether it was someone at the gas station or at work. Our mentality was, one of a man walking by a burning home whose occupants did not realize that the house was on fire, so he had to warn them. Warning others of coming danger and the way out of it was our job. By doing that, we could save lives.

****

Street Preaching

As foolish as it may sound to a dying man, to the one who is getting saved, the gospel is the power of God (1 Corinthians 1:18). That was the mentality we had when we stood out there on the corner preaching. Street preaching is radical. The church today puts down this kind of radical Christianity. It is not comfortable for many to stand on the street corner and preach. Preaching to Christians is not the same as preaching out there on the street corners. But the power of God that shows up on that street corner makes all the difference in the world.

Street preaching is a lost art in the church today. God had one Son and He was a street preacher. As he walked around the cities and towns, He was heard declaring, "Repent for the kingdom of God is near!" John the Baptist did the same and so did Peter who preached and three thousand people got saved. They lifted up their voices. The church was radical in the book of Acts and so was my church.

Perhaps the church has the imagery of the battle reversed. When the Bible talked about the "gates of hell" not prevailing against the church, that is not a defensive posture but an offensive one. The church is supposed to be kicking down the walls of hell and rescuing the lost, not cowering inside its buildings while hell is pounding on the door! But we have become domesticated. We were meant to be like lions. And lions are never tamed.

****

Our church had an aggressive Christianity and punk rock-like attitude that I loved. The group of guys from the church that I hung out with had the same wild tenacity I had in punk rock – it was all the way. And we were all the way for Jesus. We could hardly wait for the services to be over so we could go out to practice and share the word that we heard. The street corner of Whittier and Atlantic Avenue was "our pulpit," where we preached to the passersby. "Conquer the world for Jesus!" was our heart's cry.

One time while street preaching, I felt the leading of the Holy Spirit to go into a Hispanic bar. No one there spoke English.

I reminded the Lord, "God, I don't speak Spanish."

He instructed, "Keep walking."

At the end of the bar sat a white guy.

I heard the Lord say, "Go and tell that backslider to come home." I did.

The man wept as he asked, "How did you know?"

Another time, while driving home from work, the Lord told me to go to a certain corner and start preaching. Okay. For forty minutes or so, I preached – and some people opposed me while others thanked me. I felt like Noah who preached and no one got saved. But I was operating out of obedience. That Sunday, I found out why.

One of the new-convert teachers came up to me and asked, "Can I tell you something?"

I said, "Sure."

"A few days ago," he began, "I was sitting at a gar station and I wanted to quit. I wanted to throw in the towel because I did not think I was making a difference. As I opened the door of my car, I heard someone preaching. I looked around and saw that it was you. And God spoke to me and said, "You made a difference in that life."

That floored me. And it only strengthened my faith in God and being obedient to witness and proclaim the gospel.

Being such radical witnesses meant that crazy things happened all the time when we went out to witness. Outreaches in the middle of the night were part of our lifestyle. After home Bible studies at night, we combed the back streets of Los Angeles for people to talk to about Jesus. We crashed many parties by sneaking in and witnessing or praying for people. There were people we witnessed to while they were doing drugs late at night. Some got saved and others became instantly sober as we prayed for them.

One time, we ran into two cholo gang members who began to weep and cry as I witnessed to them. They felt that they could not come to God because they were high. So God instantly sobered them up after I prayed with them. Twenty minutes later, one of them was interpreting for me in Spanish as I preached the gospel.

Often, because I was the guy who got sidetracked or pulled away from the group to witness to someone, I found myself left behind. Once, while witnessing in a rough neighborhood of Los Angeles as part of an outreach for a baby church there, I saw a group of Chicano gang members far down in the alley. Leaving my group, I headed toward the gang members. Right away, I sensed their apprehension because they did not know who I was or what I wanted. I was a white guy coming in their territory. Was I on drugs or did I want to fight?

Immediately, I made my peace with them and said, "No, no, I am with the church and I wanted to tell you that Jesus loves you."

They were smoking crack and getting high. Sitting down, I began to witness to them while they passed the crack cocaine and the joint around. I told them that what they were doing didn't bother me.

"God wants to touch you man," I explained.

For twenty minutes I pleaded with them, "Jesus can set you free. He did this for me."

They were listening and getting loaded. Just then a cop pulled up in his police car and the whole group took off. I started running with them (no way was I waiting around to explain to the cop, nor was I letting the fish get away).

We were running and jumping fences, when one of them turned and asked, "Dude, why are you coming with me for?"

I hollered back, "Because I want to witness to you guys. As soon as we ditch this cop, I want to pray for you."

After hurdling over a few more fences and hiding behind trashcans, we were safe from the cop. Moments later, I prayed the sinner's prayer with them, even though some of them were loaded – they were so scared that they decided to repent.

Running down the alley to witness to that guy was crazy. No way would I advise this — run from a cop and follow someone who was doing drugs. Nor would I put it in a book on "How to Win the Lost."

At the moment when I was doing it, especially when I prayed for them, it sure felt right. Now that I think about it, I probably would not have done it. Then, it was just a matter of faith. I viewed that situation this way: I was nothing but a punk rocker who got saved. I ran from the cops as a sinner and running from a cop as a Christian was not an issue. I lived on the edge, took crazy risks as a punk rocker and even went into the dark places for the enemy. Why not do the same for God?

****

Hardcore Evangelism

I saw the punk rocker attitude in the book of Acts. It intrigued me that the disciples ran from the Pharisees. They were being chased and thrown in prison. I thought, "Man, these guys were hardcore. They were not afraid, for they were pretty tough." They stood for what they believed in.

When I ran after the gang members in the alley, it reminded me of the scripture when Jesus talked about the lost sheep in Matthew 18.

"Take heed that you do not despise one of these little ones, for I say to you that in heaven their angels always see the face of My Father who is in heaven. For the Son of Man has come to save that which was lost. What do you think? If a man has a hundred sheep, and one of them goes astray, does he

not leave the ninety-nine and go to the mountains to seek the one that is straying? And if he should find it, assuredly, I say to you, he rejoices more over that sheep than over the ninety-nine that did not go astray. Even so it is not the will of your Father who is in heaven that one of these little ones should perish (Matthew 18:10-14)."

God's heart is that of a good shepherd. He seeks after the lost and restores them to safety. He does not want anyone to perish but that all should come to repentance. He will do whatever it takes to rescue a lost sheep. If it means Him leaving the ninety-nine and going out to find the one who is lost, so be it. He climbs the mountains, looks in the crevices in the rocks and down the cliffs – the risky places. Finding that lost one is a cause for celebration and He returns it to the safety of the ninety-nine. To leave the comfort of the fold does not mean that the ninety-nine leave the fold. Knowing that the ninety nine percent are safe is not good enough for God. He wants the hundred percent! A wolf roams out there. And its goal is bigger than making people sick. The enemy's number one goal is to keep people from God.

We are the only people who have the answer to heaven. Sometimes I look at Christianity and I am reminded of a scene from the movie *The Matrix*. Morpheus was giving Neo a choice – take the blue pill and follow Him, or take the red pill and stay lost. Jesus offers us a choice and that is to follow him or not. For those who follow, Jesus promised, "Follow me and I will make you fishers of men."

Now, I like fishing and I go fishing in the lake in my back yard. I use different baits depending on the fish or the conditions for fishing. If it is too hot, I use a different lure to bring that fish to the top of the water, than when it is cold. The same applies to witnessing. Whether I am talking to someone in their office or out on the street, I have to be at their level. Sometimes those places are pretty wicked and bad.

Are we willing to adjust to that? Are we willing to go to the risky places to witness to someone? How bad do we want to see a soul won for Jesus?

****

Just Do It!

Hearing sermons about Jesus raising the dead and men like Smith Wigglesworth were inspiring and exciting. Our pastor encouraged us to go and pray for people and to expect miracles when we do. He told us that we had the power of God inside us and that Jesus said we could do greater things than He did. Those messages rang in my heart and fueled the fire of God that burnt in me.

I was still working for my father at the time. Dad and I had done some mechanic work and we were returning to his shop when we saw Otto run toward us. Otto was German and a mechanic at dad's shop. He was running and speaking frantically in English and German, and pointing to a vehicle in the road. We had barely noticed the car.

"That man is dead! He's passed out. He's not breathing!" Otto was saying. "I already called the paramedics about twenty minutes ago and they are still not here."

Exiting Dad's vehicle quickly, we ran toward the man. Dad's shop was located where there was rarely any traffic, and it was sort of bizarre that no traffic went through during that whole ordeal.

With the Smith Wigglesworth sermon still fresh in my heart, I grabbed the man and commanded, "I rebuke this spirit of death. I command you to go in the name of Jesus. Life, come into him!"

My dad and I continued to pray over him. We were praying, and I was rebuking death and nothing was happening. I'm not a doctor so I could not tell whether he was alive or dead, but all I know was that the man was neither breathing nor moving. Soon, a cop pulled up and he saw us, two big men leaning over this man, praying. Both of us had lain over this man from the passenger's side (dad's six-foot-five frame and my six-foot-two frame) and we were praying hard.

He demanded, "What are you guys doing?"

Ignoring the cop, we kept praying for a little while longer before my dad reluctantly stepped back. I kept praying.

That cop grabbed me. "Hey, get off of him!" he yelled. "Get off of him!"

But I wouldn't let go of the man. I was holding on to him.

"I rebuke this spirit. I speak life. Devil you are a liar!" Then I said again to the unresponsive man, "In Jesus' name I command you to live!"

Suddenly, the man coughed and opened his eyes. The cop freaked out.

The guy came to and cried out, "Oh my God!"

He saw me right in his face praying. Saliva was still running down his mouth from being unconscious for so long. Being a new convert, I carried the tracts called "The Big Question." The question being, "If you start reading this tract and die, where will you spend eternity?"

Nimbly placing the tract in the guy's shirt pocket, I told him, "Dude, Jesus just brought you back."

By now the cop had succeeded in pulling me off the man just as the ambulance arrived. It took the man away.

Whatever became of that guy is still a mystery to me. Was he clinically dead? I don't know. One thing I was certain of, he was unconscious and was not breathing, but when we prayed for him, he came to. His eyes opened and he breathed again at the name of Jesus.

Praying for people was something we were eager to do. We looked for opportunities to do that and we constantly found them. In the case of that man we prayed for, praying was our first response. Not that we should not call doctors or the ambulances but at the same time, we can give faith a chance. Jesus said that we will lay hands on the sick and they will recover (Mark 16:18).

This was all before I became a pastor. I was just a Christian, and a disciple that believed that God could use my life. I had the Holy Spirit that enables me to do things like that. With God within me, I knew that I could do anything. Fear was not even a factor.

****

Got Salt?

Two men were on their way to the temple. It was time to pray. This was their life and practice. Peter and John were two men who had discovered their purpose. But right before them was a lame man. He was looking to them, begging for help and provision (Acts 3). This was a hurting soul. For the two men, there was no deliberation about what to do. Neither did they pretend the lame man was not there. They simply knew that the Spirit of God within them had what the lame man needed.

Peter boldly said, "Look at us." In a way he was saying, "When you look at me, you will find someone who has compassion. Don't follow me, but follow Jesus. When you look at me, you will find Jesus."

Peter said that neither he nor John had silver or gold (verse 6). He was not lying. He had no money for that guy that day. But his lack of earthly riches to give away did not mean that he was not going to release what he had – the healing power of God. Peter knew that the man needed a miracle and not money.

"Rise and walk!" Peter said to the lame man.

Then Peter reached out and helped the man up to his feet until he received the strength to stand on his own. The once lame man began to praise God (Acts 3:8).

Ever come across someone begging for money? Have you ever told them "I have no money" when in fact you did not want to give them any? Lying to avoid dealing with the needy should not be our response. We carry an anointing from the Holy Spirit to demonstrate the power of God to the world just as Peter and John did.

The hurting people of the world are reaching up for help. A disciple's hands need to be reaching down to help them. Though the world hides their pain behind their jokes and pride, they are hurting deep down. The world needs the compassionate heart of Jesus to be released from His disciples. Because within the heart of everyone is a gap that is only reserved for the Lord alone. Are you aware of any hands reaching up to you for help lately?

Peter and John had given the lame man what they had – the life-giving gospel of Jesus. They obeyed Jesus' command to "go into all the world and preach the gospel to every creature (Mark 16:15, 16). The signs followed them because they believed (Mark 16:26-18). Peter and John's light shone that day so that when others saw their good works, they glorified their Father in heaven! Can you imagine the joy in Peter and John when they saw the lame man healed? The grateful man was so ecstatic about his healing that he was willing to follow the disciples anywhere. He went with them into the temple.

This miracle happened outside the temple building – just as the lost souls we see daily are outside the four walls of our church buildings. As would any lost and hurting soul, they expect to get something from those going to the church, or who claim to know God. The world expects something from the church. Though they see our steeples, bumper stickers and T-shirts with Christian messages, they are looking for something deeper than that – they are searching for answers. But as they look, they find that for the most part, the church looks just like the world. Those entering the church buildings carry the same values, act the same way as they do. There is no obvious separation. But we are called to be separate from the world.

The best way to build the kingdom of God is not what we are doing within our churches but on the outside of them. There is more to Christianity than just getting people into the church. We are meant to be the salt of the earth. Salt is a preserving agent. Where is our flavor?

Twenty years ago, the church was a lot different than it is now. Of course we can't completely blame the church. But now we have a different approach when presenting the gospel. Paranoia dominates our message because we are careful not to hurt people's feelings. We are apologetic for our message of life. Whatever happened to the understanding that our sharing the gospel is letting people "know the truth" and seeing that truth make them free? Sure our culture is different too. But it seemed like in our effort to adapt to the culture, we have lied and compromised the gospel. We can be relevant without changing the message.

■■■

Pushing the Edge

Dressed up as a dead gang member, I was laid in a coffin and propped up on the street. There was a fake bullet hole on my chest to make it look like I had died from a gunshot wound. This was part of our drama and outreach. While I was lying there playing dead, a group of gang members walked by and one of them looked in the coffin. For a few seconds, his face had a frightened look as if I reminded him of someone or something. Though they hurried away, I watched where they went – straight into one of the nearby apartments. Jumping out of the coffin, I followed them and knocked on the door (remember I still looked "dead" with the gunshot wound and fake blood).

A girl answered. In the background, I heard a guy asking who was at the door. Then the guy I was following looked out.

When he saw me, he had the same shocked look briefly before he got a hold of himself and asked, "Who are you?"

I replied, "I am you."

Then I proceeded to tell him, "This is how you will look if you do not turn your life around and follow Jesus." He became all ears. I began to share the gospel with him and his girlfriend. They repented and accepted the Lord. Later on, I found out that when he saw me in that coffin, I reminded him of his gangster friend who was shot and killed. Disturbing memories made him consider his own mortality.

Preaching the gospel became my life. I did so at every opportunity and open door. Once, I was with a young couple and we were driving home from church in their Toyota truck. We decided to drive into the projects. As we did, a cop drove up and shone his light on us. Could it be because of our hair? We all had crazy hair then. As far as we knew, we weren't breaking any laws.

On a hunch my friend commented, "I think the cop thinks we were doing something wrong." At the same time, he reached over to get his registration from the glove box.

"Driver, stick your hands up where we can see you!" That was the police speaking. "Driver, get out of the car!"

My friend stopped and cooperated. Immediately, eight cop cars and a helicopter arrived. They grabbed him and put him on the ground.

"Passenger, on the floor, get out!" The woman got out of the car and they put her face to the ground too. Then it was my turn.

"Passenger, get out of the car."

I told the Lord, "God, this is happening for a reason."

I exited the car still clutching my Bible.

One of the cops demanded, "What is that in your hand?"

"It's my Bible," I replied.

They pushed me facedown on the ground but I refused to let go of my Bible.

On display like that to the whole neighborhood, they got a good look at us. "It was not them," informed the neighbors. The cops apologized and released us.

We did not have the mindset of a victim. Pulling out a track, I witnessed to the cops while they stood there with their mouths open. When we turned around, we saw that a crowd had gathered. We seized the opportunity to preach the gospel, and we stayed there and ministered to the people until one o'clock in the morning. Afterward, we found out that about thirty minutes before we drove in, a white truck was driving around the neighborhood and someone in there was randomly shooting around.

Unforgettable moments like that happened all the time. One night after Bible conference, some of the guys and I ventured out for tacos at a taco stand. But we were more eager to see souls saved than for those tacos. We came across some backsliders and began to witness to them. I noticed a guy on an Intercepter motorcycle and I walked over and told him that Jesus loved him. He mocked me. I told him that there was a reason that I was telling him that because his life was like a vapor.

"You could pull out of this parking lot tonight and die," I said.

He laughed at me and pulled out of the parking lot. Just then, a car came by and hit him. In my mind, this could be his last chance if he was still alive. I ran over and witnessed to him some more. Some of the guys with me joined me as we prayed for him.

Could it be that God would send us to people with their last chance? I'll never know. But I was sure that I had chosen to live a Spirit-led life. I don't know whether that man lived or died, but I will never forget that incident. If he died and did not receive salvation, he will live in eternal regret.

****

Are You My Neighbor?

Beating him within inches of death, the thieves stripped the man of everything and then took off (Luke 10:30). Right afterward, two men, a priest (a spiritual man) and a Levite (one who offers sacrifice) came by, saw the wounded man and crossed the street to avoid him. Both saw the man lying there, all bloodied and beat up. They were in too much of a hurry and too busy to stop. Tending to that dying man would take a while – time they did not want to waste on him. Also, they did not want their nice church clothes soiled! They were sure someone else was coming along soon. Wasn't this a busy street anyway (Luke 10: 31, 32)?

Fortunately for the wounded man, a Samaritan man came by just in time to save his life. Compassion compelled the Samaritan to tend to the wounded man. Getting off his donkey (his high horse if you will), he humbled himself and bandaged the man's wounds, pouring oil and wine (representing the Holy Spirit) on his injuries. After that, he placed him on his donkey and carried him to the safety of an inn.

He provided the hurting man physical and spiritual healing.

Showing compassion may mean more than just tending to the immediate needs of the hurting. It may mean carrying the wounded for a while until they heal. The inn where the wounded man lay while he recovered could be like the church. Our attitude should be like the Samaritan man offering to pay for and see the wounded recover. We must be willing to do whatever it takes to see someone get saved. Sadly, the people in the world sometimes seem to have more compassion for the hurting, than those in the church.

What prompted that story? Someone had asked Jesus, "What must I do to inherit eternal life?" Jesus began to tell the story of being a good neighbor. According to the illustration, a good neighbor is "The one who had compassion."

Right away, Jesus urged his listener to "Go and do likewise."

The story of the "Good Samaritan" illustrated a fascinating point that intrigued me today – the church is on the wrong side of the street! It seems to me that the most religious people (churchgoers) had forgotten where they came from. Building our churches in the suburbs where people have their families together is more comfortable. This is something I have to guard my heart against, even as a young disciple.

Part of our acts of Christianity in reaching the lost is, to take what we learn in the house of God out into the streets. Yes, we need to pray and read the word, but we must not forget to reach out to the lost world. Discipleship includes your Christianity in action – help someone else. We cannot do that if we are crossing over to the wrong side of the street.

****

"I have the same Jesus that you have!" declared the pastor at the Christian crusade.

One of my best friends, Abraham Pedraja, and I were inspired by that message. We felt led to go out and compel others to come to Jesus. Who could we reach? Then we remembered the people in the olive trees. The family of Abraham's wife had a house in Mexico (two hours from the border of the United States and Mexico). We had heard that there were hurting people living in the olive trees near there. After we asked our pastor if we could we go and pray for these people, a group of us drove there. We went with the blessing of our leaders. None of them went with us.

What we saw as we drove up the dirt road was heart-wrenching for our group who had come from the land of plenty – the United States of America. Homes were made in the trees and bushes. Water was fetched from the trenches. We began to cry. There was no doubt in our minds that this was what we were supposed to do. After having observed what our Pastor had done in the past, we knew what to do. We passed out Bibles, and then stood on our van and preached. We prayed for anyone who was sick that day, and we saw goiters and lumps disappear, and ears and eyes opened. Hundreds of people began to get saved. We did not want to leave them there. So, the next day, we drove back to the olive groves and packed our van with people and drove it to the nearest Praise Chapel.

The Pastor there said, "Where did these people come from?"

"From the olive grove," we answered.

"That is funny," the Pastor said with a thoughtful look, "Last week, the Lord put it on my heart to start a Bible study there and now you brought all these people here."

Indeed, we heard of a need and we went.

****

God's Heart for the Lost

The invitations are out for everyone to that great feast (Luke 14:15-24). His servants are out with the invitations and the Master is waiting for the replies. But the responses are less than disheartening to the Master – they are infuriating. With one excuse after the other, the ones invited were too busy or too committed elsewhere. So the Master extends the invitation to those on the streets and lanes, the poor, the crippled the blind and lame.

Sometimes the hardest of the lost to win, may not be those on drugs, alcohol, in rebellion or caught up in some perversion, but it may be those who are normal. It may be the ones with a good marriage and jobs, nice families, and with no financial problems. These are the ones who go to church and have a form of religion but have not surrendered to God. Those are usually the hardest ones to get saved. The Master gave a chance to such people but their excuses caused Him to go to the rejected and the broken of society.

Oh that we would have the heart of God for the lost! As comfortable as it is to hang around other Christians, that is part of it. We are already saved, our lives are already changed and we are going to heaven. Out there is a world of lost people who are dying. We must never forget that.

My biggest passion is winning souls and getting people saved. The church that I got saved in was a soul-winning church. My pastor instilled a motto inside my heart; "We want those that nobody else wants. If you don't want them in your church, we will take them." God really honored that. We wanted to reach the hurting and the lost.

Everyone wants a miracle, but we have to need one first. If we want healing, we have to be sick first! Victory does not come unless we are in some sort of defeat. For deliverance to come, we must first know that we are bound. When we look for that financial blessing, we must first have a financial need. To be found, we must be truly lost. These are the economies of the kingdom of God.

****

CHAPTER THREE

Training for Life

Imitating Albert

Living close to Albert was God-ordained, especially for discipleship. From the time I asked him to help me learn to pray and read the Bible, Albert began to disciple me. Albert was a good teacher. He imparted to me a love for the word of God. Many times, I sat with him at his table, while he taught me how to read the Bible (I was barely able to read and I did not do well in school). He showed me how to study it. To understand many of the words in the Bible (I did not know many of them), he showed me how to use a dictionary. Later, he added a concordance and then finally a Bible commentary. The Bible became the first book in my life that I enjoyed reading. It went everywhere with me so that I could read it every possible moment. And the more I read the Bible and heard the word of God preached, the more I realized what I had to change in my life.

Church was a place to learn – this was what I was taught. Listen and take notes. I always took a paper and pen to church services. There was a growing hunger for the Word of God in my life. Jesus' words that said "Man shall not live by bread alone but by every word that proceeds from the mouth of God," was a truth I was discovering.

Prayer was another important thing in Albert's life. He began to teach me how to pray. We started with the basics. He instructed me to kneel next to him when he prayed and to listen to how he prayed. Later, I learned that what Albert did was no different from how Jesus taught his disciples to pray (Luke 11:1). Jesus was literally instructing his disciples to say the words that he was saying when he told them, "When you pray, say..." and then he taught them the Lord's Prayer (Luke 11:2-4). Albert's habits of rising early to pray and going to pray before church services were habits I learned to imitate. He instilled in me a heart committed to prayer. Because I hung around a man of God who taught me how to pray I was baptized with the Holy Ghost three weeks after salvation.

It was a year later. He must have thought that I was ready. Countless hours have been spent reading and studying the Bible with Albert. He asked me if I wanted to teach a Bible study. The joy of finally being able to do something I desired was mixed with anxiety. Albert took me step by step on how to prepare a Bible Study. He helped me put the message together. Then he had me preach it to him (to break the ice). Fasting all week was part of it. Fasting was also a part of what Albert taught me how to do, and Friday was the day we fasted.

On the night of the Bible study Albert introduced me "Today we have a special blessing," he said. "Kelly is going to share with us tonight."

At that moment, I felt like a Jewish man being handed a scroll to read and teach. I was terrified. The message was about stretching your faith. I talked about the story of Abraham and Isaac. The message lasted about ten minutes (yes, I fasted all week for a ten minute message). Little did I know that preaching and teaching the Word of God would be my life's calling. But that night, I sweated from the anxiety of having to teach. Thankfully, the families that were there that night loved and accepted me so that it somewhat eased my discomfort.

****

Discipleship 101

He found life. This beggar was no longer confined to the temple grounds. He was free to go wherever he wanted. After this wonderful miracle though, the once lame man did not want to let go of Peter and John. In fact, he clung to Peter's tunic (Acts 3:11). He wanted to be near them. The whole scene had attracted a crowd and provided Peter an opportunity to preach the gospel (Acts 3:17-26). But they had already gained a disciple – the healed beggar who hung on their every word.

Three types of relationships need to be active in the life of every believer. One is a spiritual father, two is peer relations and three is discipleship. Promise Keepers got a hold of this truth. Thus, their statement that, "every man needs a Paul, every man needs a Barnabas and every man needs a Timothy." Paul urged believers to follow him as he followed Christ. We are called to always be disciples, no matter where we are as a Christian. That means in our lives, we need someone to hold onto who is always teaching us and imparting into our lives. At the same time, I must have someone holding onto me that I teach. Paul imparted into Timothy and Titus. He said, "I have begotten you as sons in the faith." As a spiritual father, Paul poured his life into them. The Bible has several examples: Joshua had Moses, Elisha had Elijah, Peter had Jesus and Timothy had Paul.

Peer relationships are just as important. We never get to a place where we cannot allow anyone to speak into our lives. Every disciple needs a peer. Barnabas was a peer of Paul, and Peter had John. Each of these two shared a common level in their relationships with God. Ecclesiastes talks about the benefits of having two people working together instead of one. The same principle works when believers gather – two gathering in His name guarantees that Jesus is there in their midst. Two can agree on anything. Just as we need spiritual fathers and people to disciple, we also need a peer, someone running alongside us, as an encourager. I would not be here today if it weren't for the Barnabas in my life, my friends who told me not to quit.

Imparting into someone else's life is something we can do as believers. Every man needs a Timothy or someone who he can impart his life and faith into. So not only are they receiving from a spiritual father, they also have an outlet. Otherwise they risk stagnation in their walk with God. It is a matter of "freely receive, freely give." This gospel is too great for us to keep to ourselves. Jesus' last words were "to go into the world and make disciples." That means something. Those last words were not the least important but rather, they should be foremost and urgent in our minds. That is the way to live life.

****

Discovering Esther

I never noticed her at first. Esther was very close to her brother. They practically always had their arms around each other (not in a perverted way) and gave each other a kiss on the cheek. People thought that they were married because they were always together and sat next to each other. Her family was a close-knit Latino one that was highly affectionate. Later, I found out about Esther's crazy testimony and that explained why the family appeared close to outsiders. Her brother, Albert, had his child kidnapped from by his ex-wife, so he was wounded, and Esther had left an abusive relationship. Dating was out of the question. They just served God and protected each other.

Esther's first impression of me when I first came to church was more of pity than anything. As a newly saved young man, I was skinny and sickly looking from drugs, and my eyes were sunken in. In fact, because I could hardly speak (my brain was fried from the drug abuse), Esther thought that I was retarded.

Oh that poor guy! she thought. *We need to pray for him so that he makes it.*

Slowly, my mind started clearing up. As I became more stable and sane, I noticed her like I would notice anyone else. Esther sang in the choir and was always in the prayer room. But it was not long before our paths collided.

One day, we had an outreach to San Francisco for one of our baby churches. Rudy Trujillo was the pastor there. A band called Ekklesia (Brother Albert was the lead singer and lead guitar player) was playing for the outreach and our church drama group was assigned to do the dramas in downtown San Francisco. Esther and I were both part of this drama team. Our team rode together to San Francisco in a fifteen-passenger van. Talking to Esther came naturally for me during that long ride and I did not think anything of it.

The first drama we had to perform was about the Great White Throne of God and because of the schedule, our team made the trip down to San Francisco in our costumes. I played Gay Gary from San Francisco, who was not a flamboyant homosexual but a rude one (I was willing to do anything if it was for God). No one in the church knew that we had dressed like we were for the drama. When I entered the building, the ushers began to witness to me. But I acted rebellious. I would not even clap my hands during worship - and that was all part of the play. Esther played Juicy Lucy, a Madonna-type girl (that was when Madonna was a big deal). We really got into those parts or at least tried. Then the drama began.

Imagine everyone's surprise when my turn came in the play and they called out, "Gay Gary, your time has come!"

I stood up and said, "Hey, that's me!"

A second drama we did was about a biker couple. Esther and I got to play the married couple. I was nervous because Esther had been on the drama team for a while and she was really good at acting.

Seeing my nervousness, she pointed to her sides and suggested, "Just grab me right here." I did just that and then threw her against the wall and pretended to beat her up (all part of the drama). But we still did not think anything of it.

One day, I went to Albert's place (Esther's brother) to get a haircut. Albert had cut hair for many years and was very good at it. It was a common thing for him to cut many peoples' hair from our church. Some people thought that I had ulterior motives for going to Albert's house, like seeing Esther for instance but I truly didn't — at least not yet. Esther was there. Afterwards, I was going to the mall and Esther wanted to go with me. This caused quite a stir in her family for they began talking very loudly and fast Cuban Spanish (I did not know much Spanish then like I do now) and were saying things to her that I didn't understand. I had no clue that they were mad and discouraging her from going.

"How could you go with this type of guy?" they said, besides other things. Their view of me then was not good. After all, I was white and had a less-than-appealing past.

Esther was twenty at the time and so was I. Despite all the flack her family gave her for going with me, she went anyway. I did not think anything about it. But after that trip to the mall, I started thinking about Esther. I liked her. That was when I started praying for her.

After a while, I went to Pastor Neville "Hey Pastor, I want to ask you a question," I said. "I have been thinking about this girl in church."

He kindly asked, "Who have you been thinking and praying about?"

I answered, "Esther Garcia."

"Kelly, she is a good girl." he said, "You pray and fast about it and then come and we'll talk again."

I also told the associate pastor, Woody Calvary. I asked him, "How do I know if this is the woman of God for me or not?"

Pastor Woody was frank, "Just fast and pray about it for five days. God will speak to you."

I said, "Okay." This did not seem very hard at all. I started the next day.

The first two days, I went without water. This was fasting to "kill my flesh" (Galatians 5:24).

Later, I found out that Esther was praying for me at the same time. She had talked to the pastor's wife about me.

Back in those days in our church, doing the will of God was above everything else. Someone who wanted to serve God wholeheartedly couldn't just marry anybody. Making sure the person you wanted to marry desired to serve God too was top priority. Since I knew that I was called to preach the gospel, this was very important to me. The woman I would marry needed to be someone who wanted to serve God with me. Beauty was not a main factor.

Esther.

She was a faithful woman and had a heart to serve God. She was in the choir, the drama team, always in the prayer room, attended Bible Study, went on outreaches and prayed at the altar – she was everything I wanted my wife to be. She met my requirements for a wife. For her, when she saw me street preaching, she began to look at me differently. God spoke to her about me and so she started to pray.

Finally I mustered up enough courage to talk to Esther.

After one Sunday night service, I walked up to her and said, "Hey, can I talk to you?" I walked really straight with a militant posture (that was the approach back then). "Can we step outside?"

I was nervous. This was my first solid and hardcore conversation with her.

But I am not a man who beats around the bush. "Hey," I said. "I have been praying and fasting for you. I feel that God showed me that we should get married…if you want to get married." (I pretty much told her that I liked her and wanted to marry her in the same conversation). Esther was speechless.

Twenty feet from us stood her dad, who kept glancing at his watch as he glared at me. No doubt he was wondering what I was telling his daughter. He did not look happy.

So I kept talking, "I feel like we should get married. I believe this is God's will. If you don't like me in that way, let me know and I'll leave you completely alone." It was take it or leave it.

Of course, my heart was coming out of my chest. I was thinking, *This is crazy.*

Then Esther spoke "No, I've been praying for you too."

And my heart went, "Yes!"

That is how we hooked up.

Having settled the issue of marriage in that brief conversation, hell came against our relationship – just after we went to talk to Pastor Neville the following week.

The pastor was encouraging and supportive "That is great!" he said. "You guys do good and in about six months, you can get married." Then he walked away.

I thought, *Wow that is great! We are really doing this.*

Before he left, he instructed me this way "I don't want you around her for three months. I don't want you to be alone with her. You can talk to her at church."

So that was the extent of our relationship. Esther and I talked only at church and I would call her once or twice a week.

Elsewhere in the church, some people were stirring up trouble for us. Sara, my old punker girlfriend, was still there and had not changed her feelings toward me. Another couple in the church leadership thought that I should marry her instead.

Two weeks later, a guy pulled me aside "I heard that you like Esther Garcia."

Unaware of his intentions, I replied with enthusiasm, "Yeah man, I've been praying and I feel like it is God's will."

"Esther is a whore." His statement caught me completely off guard.

"What?"

"She makes guys backslide."

Now I was alarmed "What are you talking about?"

"It's not God's will. You are supposed to be with this girl Sara." Where did this guy get his information?

I was defensive "How are you going to tell me that? I talked to Pastor Neville and he said it was good and I got his blessing."

"Pastor does not know what I know." Such a big mistake on his part!

Our conversation was over. I ended it with "Hey, I'm not going to talk to you."

Simultaneously, another leader's wife (now a pastor's wife) took Esther aside and said, "Kelly is not the kind of guy for you. He's the kind of guy that is not going to be good for you or be around. He is the kind that will cheat on you. This other guy Eddie Arnales is the one for you."

Come to find out later, the man who talked to me was Eddie's best friend! Apparently, Eddie too had been praying for Esther for a long time. No matter what people said about Esther or me, I stuck to my guns – Esther was a good woman and I intended to marry her. Some of them did not believe me and continued to talk trash about us. Sadly, those involved with this manipulating and conniving were involved in ministry.

Despite this ongoing drama, it never crossed my mind to leave the church. We did not think that way. Actually, we felt like this was the only church in town and in the world for us because of what God was doing in our lives. Even Esther's family entered this fray. Her brother tried to fix her up with other men so that she would not be with me. Constantly, they told her that I was going to backslide and that I was not going to do anything for God.

"He is the wrong guy for you," they advised her.

Her mother disliked me, to put it mildly.

"You'll never marry my daughter!" Her mother would tell me whenever I called their house to talk to Esther. Then she would hang up the phone after she yelled at me. Sometimes, she would scream at Esther and hit her. But she acted like she had done nothing wrong when she came to church. She just lifted her hands and praised God during worship.

This drama went on for seven months. I felt like Jacob and the trouble he went through with Laban before he could marry Rachel. Of course, there was no comparison there and I figured seven months was not that long to wait. (Through time, I've proven them all wrong. Her brother, who is now a pastor, apologized later saying that he was wrong, but I still tease him about it whenever I preach at his church.)

During that seven-month period, we did what we were supposed to do. We saw each other only on outreaches or when there was a church fellowship. We cherished those moments that were open and accountable. Except for that day in July when I celebrated my twenty-first birthday toward the end of the seven-month period.

"Pastor, my birthday is coming up." I needed his permission just to keep myself accountable. "Do you mind if I take Esther to Six Flags Magic Mountain for my birthday?"

He was hesitant, "Well, Kelly, you have been faithful. If you really want to."

Looking back now, I know that he did not want me to do it. He had always told me not to be alone with her. Besides I had always told him that I was not going to kiss her until I married her.

But he gave me a look that said, "Good luck."

This was my first official date with Esther, without anyone else around. I could hardly wait to be alone with her, so I picked her up really early from her mom's house. We had a forty-five-minute drive down to the Park and it was weird to have her sitting in the front seat with me. But I loved it. The park was still closed when we got there because we made the trip so early. Seeing a Burger King by the park entrance we decided to go there and buy something to eat.

We parked the car and instead of getting out, we just sat there talking. And oh it was so subtle. Our hands touched. I felt like I was with a girl for the first time despite all the junk I did before. Unable to contain myself, I found myself kissing her. Then she was in my arms. We started making out. And it was still early in the morning. During this whole time, I was so convicted. *How could this be wrong when it felt so good?* I thought.

In the distance I heard a pounding noise. I ignored it and continued to kiss Esther. Then the wind started to pick up and the nearby trees were swaying. The pounding sound was getting louder. Though I was getting nervous, I did not want to stop what I was doing. As I kissed her, I was looking out the front window of my car. The sound became deafening and the trees continued dancing and now my car was shaking. Then these wild thoughts came to mind.

"O my God, this is God telling me to stop! Was I going to lose my destiny because I was kissing Esther? Are we going to mess up?"

Suddenly, an ambulance helicopter landed right in front of the car, with the propellers close to the front of it. I'm holding Esther in my arms when the helicopter door opened and they brought out a gurney. As the emergency personnel ran by the car with the gurney, they looked at us.

I let Esther go and said, "This is God. God stopped us."

Did someone in Burger King have a heart attack so that Esther and I would stop making out? I believed they did.

A month later, Pastor Neville went to his office to meet with Esther and me. It was a well-known fact then that when two singles (male and female) walked into the Pastor's office that they were about to get married. The choir was practicing that Sunday afternoon.

The pastor said, "Listen guys. It's time to make a move." Then he addressed Esther "Kelly's got the call of God on his life. If you are not willing to go anywhere in the world with him, you can walk out of this office and leave this young man alone."

Instantly I was thinking, *Jesus, please don't let her leave.*

Such an unfounded fear! Esther was sure. "No," she said. "That is what I want to do."

Opening his calendar, the pastor said, "Fine. When do you want to get married? We need to do this quick because it is going to get too chancy."

Without thinking, I blurted out, "In two months." So our wedding was planned for October 2, 1988.

When we came out of that office, we were happy and smiling. People were looking at us. The ring! I remembered that it was still in my car.

I gestured to Esther as we walked outside "Hey, come here."

She followed me to my car. The ring was still there in the glove box where I had last put it.

"Here is your engagement ring." I said cheerfully.

Two months later, Esther and I were married during a Sunday morning service. I invited a bunch of my punker friends to the wedding. Although I loved Esther, the whole reason for my getting married was to do the will of God.

A Marriage Challenge

Esther was the right woman for me. She was beautiful and an awesome woman of God (still is). People said nothing but good things about her. But something arose in Esther a few weeks after marriage that needed to be dealt with quickly, (although it seemed to drag on for a while). Right after we got married, something changed. Something that had been dormant in her surfaced, but she did not know that it was there. It was jealousy – in an extreme form. No one saw it coming, not even me.

Esther's first marriage was a terrible one. Her first husband had abused her emotionally and physically in a very extreme way. She had even caught him in bed with another woman in her house. After her first marriage failed, she stayed close to her family but her old wound was never healed. So the first six months of our marriage seemed like hell.

Contending with Esther's jealousy was difficult. I had to do things differently because she was so paranoid that I was going to cheat on her. This became so bad that if we were at church and the pastor said, "Grab your neighbors by the hand, let's pray," and a girl was next to me, it would be a crazy situation. Esther would not let me go to the grocery store if the cashier was a girl. Sometimes after people left our house after a fellowship, she would accuse me of cheating.

"I'd seen you grab her butt and she touched you." She was hallucinating.

It got to the point where I had to put my head down in church to avoid seeing another woman or girl. Sara was still at church at this time. If she was on one side of the church, I had to be on the other. We could not join in fellowship with any of my friends. We had to go home right away. Extremely exasperated with the whole situation, I would go to the pastor crying because I did not know what to do with her.

It only worsened. During this time, a friend of mine was going to get married. A group of men were meeting at his house to pray over him and I was not going to miss it.

Esther saw me get ready and she said, "You're not going."

I insisted, "I'm sick of this. I want to go."

Her suspicion was not going to keep me home this time — I got in the car and closed the door. Esther followed me out in her underwear (no pants) and pounded on my car door.

"Let me in. You're not going! I know that you are going to do something bad."

But I ignored her and drove away. Esther instantly got on her ten-speed bike (she was still in her underwear with no pants) and followed me. I floored the accelerator.

I realized things had gone too far. I needed Esther to be free. There was a little bathroom in our garage that became my prayer place. Locking the door, I kneeled down and prayed in tongues.

Then I would cry out to the Lord, "God do a miracle! I rebuke the devil right now."

Clearly at my wits' end, I went again to Pastor Neville and said, "Pastor, I don't know what to do."

He looked at me and asked, "How bad is it?"

My face was telltale of my misery. "Pastor, is my marriage going to make it?"

His answer left me discouraged "I don't know. It's pretty bad."

This was the man I looked to for faith and inspiration, my spiritual father, and he was not sure. Things were looking rather bleak for my marriage.

"You're not supposed to say that," I groaned.

He explained, "Kelly, I've never seen jealousy like this in my life."

Nothing seemed to be working, not even counseling with Pastor Neville and Pastor Donna. In fact, Esther seemed more possessive. Within those six months, I lost all my friends in the church because I could not be with them. We could not go out in public. We went to church and then home right away. Going to outreaches was out of the question, especially if she was not going or if girls were there. I had to go with my friends and be very clear about it. Pastor Neville said that I could not do anything for God if she was like that, or teach Bible study.

Marrying Esther was not a mistake, but in my heart I cried out, "Oh God, I did not see this coming." Looking back now, the whole situation seemed comical (even Esther thinks so), but while it happened, it was pure misery.

Several things began to happen to set my wife free. One was a word from Pastor Donna Neville.

"Esther," she counseled, "you need to be very careful. What you keep speaking and envisioning over your husband, you might just speak this over his life. And it would be your fault."

Immediately, something snapped in Esther and she replied, "Oh no, I don't want this."

So Esther too began to contend against this evil in her life. It reminded me of the green Bugs Bunny. I could tell when she was assaulted by it because she would have a strange look on her face.

Sometimes during worship, when I glanced over and saw that she had that look, I would ask her, "Are you okay?"

"No, the devil is lying to me," she whispered and then she would go to the bathroom and pray over her head rebuking the evil thoughts.

For a while, whenever Esther felt this thing come on her at church, she would go to the restroom to pray and rebuke the devil. She had to fight and fight until it left her.

Getting rid of an old ring that Esther wore was another key to Esther's freedom. In the midst of this, a pastor from Puerto Rico was visiting and he saw Esther's ring.

"Let me see that ring." Then he inquired, "Where did you get it?"

"It was my grandmother's" she replied. Her grandmother was a witch or a Santaria (witch doctor with a mixture of Catholicism mostly found in the Caribbean).

He said, "Let me show you something."

He took the ring, twisted and turned it to show a secret chamber that was filled with powder. Destroying that ring was the beginning of deliverance in our home. At the same time, I would pray and fast for her. It was not instantaneous. She fought and contended for freedom from that thing. Eventually, Esther was free.

When God Called Albert

Albert influenced my faith in my first years as a believer. After all, he discipled me as a new convert. It was natural for me to want to be like him. I was like Albert's shadow. Everything Albert did (Bible studies, visit people, witness), I wanted to do. Imagine my hurt when the day came for that to end. For the first time after being saved, I had a hard time letting go (2 Timothy 2:3).

It was a Friday night service. For some reason, Albert was dressed very nice. That should have been a clue – one I got later. In those days, the Praise Chapel conference was the place where announcements for those pioneering new work were announced. Everyone else is supposed to be surprised except, of course, the couple being sent out. Pastor was announcing couples who were being sent out to pioneer churches.

"And Albert and Yolanda are going to Irving, Texas!"

Everyone shouted for joy. Texas! Now that was a far move, and oh so sudden too (at least for me)! I was angry and I began to cry. Emotions and questions welled up within me. How could he leave me? I couldn't do this without him. But Albert did not seem to notice. He and Yolanda walked right by me as I cried. And just like that, Albert was gone.

I did not talk to Albert for days. His family was preparing to move to Texas. A realization dawned on me. Although I loved Pastor Michael Neville, my pastor did not disciple me but rather Albert. Pastor Neville imparted into his Bible study leader (Albert), who then imparted into my life. Now it was time for me to rise up. Only after Albert had left, I realized that I had become a disciple. It reminded me of the story of the Karate Kid, when he was being trained. Chores such as painting the fence and learning to "wax on and wax off" were frustrating for him because his idea of being trained was not the same as his teacher's. That is discipleship. Everything counts. Even Albert's departure was part of my discipleship. For him just to pick up his family and move to a city that he did not know, to do the will of God, was a major lesson.

Soon after, opportunities opened up for me to be a substitute Bible study leader. Several of us were substitutes. There were about fifty home Bible studies in the church, which were broken up into teams. Even with that many Bible study leaders, things would happen such as leaders having to work late or being sick and we had to fill in. To get a call,

"We need you to teach somewhere," was exciting. I felt like an evangelist.

In the process of time, the friends I was saved with all became Bible study leaders, except for me. I struggled with that. Though I never felt overlooked, I always wondered why. God had a timing that I did not understand. Every time my friends were announced to be a Bible study leader, I was happy for them but I wanted a chance to do it myself. But that was missing the mark. We are in this for Jesus, and not for ourselves. Talk about a difficult lesson (today some people feel held back by the pastor and the leaders when, in reality, the timing is not right.). Those were such bittersweet moments!

****

Foundations of Discipleship

These are the five principles that were preached and built into my life as a disciple.

1. Pray
2. Read your Bible
3. Come faithfully to the house of God
4. Witnessing to others outside the church
5. Giving – not just tithing

We have lost the concept of being a true disciple. Even the phrase "discipleship" for some conjures up images and shouts of "too dogmatic" or "too religious." But we are not meant to raise Christians.

Jesus asked us to make disciples. He also said that we would do greater things than He did. How awesome is that?

Paul encouraged Timothy in this: that what he (Timothy) heard from Paul, he was meant to commit them to faithful men. Not just any men, but those who are able to teach others (2 Timothy 2:2). Timothy was expected to pour out into the life of faithful men. Then the faithful men were expected to teach others. It was about four generations of passing down the faith. What a far cry from Christianity today! For the most part, it is not a case of the churches not being fed but rather, the people are refusing to eat.

When we learn to be hungry for the things of God, we nurture that childlike faith. We are always ready and willing to believe God. As a new convert, hearing God's word preached was like a roller coaster ride – I fastened my seatbelt and hung on for the ride of my life. But I always was eager to get back on and go for another ride. Pastor Neville's preaching, and those of others were molding and shaping me. But I did not realize it. God was changing me from the inside out. My mumbling changed as I continued to go to the house of God.

Churches are meant to change us as we gather with God's people. Offenses can be forgiven. Bitterness can be uprooted. In the case of the apostles, Peter and John were a team that went out to minister together (Acts 3:1). This was the same Peter who had denied Christ and for a time suffered from the pain of denial, regret and shame. John represented people in the church who had to be willing to accept those who forsake the church but then returned in repentance. Both men went up at the hour of prayer. In regards to prayer, this was something I learned from the men of God I hung around. They were men who prayed and faithfully attended the designated prayer times at church.

****

Sidetracked

It was an opportunity to make good money and have benefits. Someone in the Bible Study who worked for Wonder Bread gave me the job lead. Without even praying about it, I took the job. Bringing in large commission checks was the upside. The downside was, I began to work fifteen to sixteen hours a day. I started work at 3 pm driving a truck and my days off were Sundays and Wednesdays. Even though I went to Bible Study, I was always exhausted. The job consumed me. This was my fork in the road. The vision God gave me for my life grew dimmer as my job became more important. There was a pull back and forth that I felt. Church challenged me but then I had to go back to my job. Something was going to have to give.

It began when Pastor Neville preached about doing the will of God. I told him that I still wanted to be a Bible study leader.

He looked at me kindly and said, "Kelly, you can't right now. You work long hours, and you don't have time to put quality time in it."

That much was true. Often, I walked into Bible Study smelling like bread. It began to sink in.

Bible conference back then was held every six months (not every other year like it is now in our fellowship of churches). Having never missed one before, with this new job, I could not make it. My wife went the first night of the conference alone. After work, I went to meet her at a restaurant later that night. Some of Esther's friends and Pastor Neville had gone there after the meeting. This was strange. I was always the one who was seen and now I was not around. It was painful being there at the restaurant listening to everyone else talking about winning the world and I was talking about a new seven-grain wheat bread!

Suddenly, one of the pastors turned and looked at me and asked, "Kelly what happened? We are talking about the bread of life and you are talking about the home pride bread."

I had no reply. He continued, "You need to quit that job tonight and come to the conference."

Now I know that this is radical. Someone reading this would think that this was controlling but in my heart, I knew this was right. I went home that night wrestling with this. I called to mind all those prayers that I had prayed in front of the fireplace, the commitment I had made on my knees before the Lord, and all that the Lord had done. Deep down, the pastor's words echoed. I knew what I had to do. Before I found the Lord, I did whatever my flesh and friends told me to do. After I got saved, I did whatever the Holy Spirit and my leaders told me to do.

At 1:30 am I called my boss (after being saved, I never quit a job without giving notice) and told him I was quitting that day. I told him that I wanted to do the will of God and be a Bible Study leader.

He was furious "Is God going to pay your bills?" he asked. "I got you a good job and a good route and you are going to throw it away for a book?"

Returning the route book for my job was not pleasant. The boss yelled at me and cussed up a storm. But I could not turn back. I was done with Wonder Bread.

Jobless, I went to conference the next day with a renewed excitement. Esther also appeared happy – and then she told me the great news. She was pregnant. We were both ecstatic. Being unemployed with a pregnant wife was not worrisome to me at that time. I figured I had a backup plan. Especially when I had a promising job interview at the end of the week.

It seemed like I had clinched the job during the interview, until a backslider who worked at that company went by the office and saw me. A day later, I received a disappointing phone call saying that I did not get the job. I found out later that the backslider told the boss not to hire me because they needed someone faithful and that I would not be. He told the boss that because I attended the Praise Chapel church, all of us who went there would eventually leave to go someplace else to pastor a church.

Down to the unemployment office I went.

The first question they asked me was, "Why did you quit your job?"

I told her because I wanted to do the will of God and teach Bible Study. The lady looked at me funny. At the end of the interview, she said I made too much money to qualify. Feeling disappointed, I trudged home. Fortunately, a brother in the church got me a job interview for the following week.

All I wanted to do was be a Bible Study leader. My thoughts were consumed with this as I stopped to get gas for my car. I remembered that I was going to pay for $5 of gas on Pump #5. By the time I turned around, someone had stolen my car! The police showed up and said that there was nothing they could do. This added insult to injury. While walking home from the gas station, the devil was tormenting me in my mind.

He said, "So you want to be a Bible Study leader? I will mess with your life. I'll kill your baby."

Arriving home, I gave Esther the disappointing news – my car was stolen, and I was also denied Medicaid and unemployment benefits.

Two weeks later, I went to my Pastor on a Wednesday afternoon, and I reported my situation. "Hey I don't know if you heard, but I lost everything — my car, my job, and I was denied unemployment! And my wife is pregnant. I'm available to teach Bible Study."

He told me, "Well Kelly, I'll keep that in mind. Hang in there."

Walking home for half a mile from church, I was not feeling very encouraged. But when I arrived home, Esther had an envelope in her hand. Then she said that I had a job offer on the phone. The job offer came with full benefits that began right away. Plus, I also had a check in the mail.

That was only the beginning. There was a service that night. Halfway through it, one of the assistant pastors told me that two men from church saw someone driving my stolen car and had chased it to downtown Los Angeles. After they got the cops involved, they got my car back. Within 24 hours, I was restored everything that the devil had stolen from me from the time I walked into the pastor's office and announced that I still wanted to teach Bible Study and do the will of God.

About a month later, a Bible Study opened up and I took over as the leader. About the same time, my wife gave birth to a baby boy. I was a father and Bible study leader. It was exciting and a blessing of being entrusted with people. The fruit from that Bible Study had been sweet. Today, one of the couples from that Bible Study is pastoring a church, and one teen girl is now married to a wonderful husband and attending my church today. Another couple is still at Huntington Park and their children are serving God. One of the families attends the Bell Gardens church, and one of the kids is a youth pastor for his dad who is pastoring a church.

It had been a long journey. But this thought always occupies my mind to this day, *God I am just a punk rocker. Are you sure you have the right guy?* As far as I know, He has not told me no.

■■

The Bottom Line

What is the kingdom of God all about? When we take away the stuff that represents our churches and ministries (electrical instruments, the programs etc.) this whole thing is about souls – people going to heaven or hell. All these other things can be fluff.

Many are on the wide road that leads to destruction. Few are choosing and finding the short and narrow road that leads to life. The opportunity to impact people's lives in the living room or on the street corner is no light thing. That is a responsibility to be taken seriously.

■■

CHAPTER FOUR

Answering the Call

Called to Be a Pastor

Clearly, the vision was sometime in the future. There I was seated on the front row of a church with pews, wearing a suit and tie (I had not worn a suit and tie to church at this point). My best friend, Abraham, a radical guy, was preaching and jumping around.

"God, is Abraham going to be my pastor?" I asked the Lord.

I heard Him say, "No. You are going to be the pastor and Abraham is going to be an evangelist preaching a revival for you." (At the time, Pastor had not ordained any evangelists from Praise Chapel).

That vision took six years to be fulfilled. But the Lord gave me that vision after about three months of being a new convert. It happened while I was on my knees praying at a Saturday morning prayer. The call to pastor began to burn in my heart, though the road to being one was still a long way away.

Not long after that, I went to my first World Bible Conference. Several thousand people from Praise Chapel filled the arena. The excitement of wanting to win the world was intoxicating and addicting. Every sermon was preached with an urgency to see people *saved*.

One particular night, when Bobby Manchaca preached about pioneering and God's plan for us to go and win souls, the fire to fulfill that call was burning in my bones. By the time the altar call came, hundreds of people ran to the altar – including me.

Within me came this cry, "God, use me. It's my life that belongs to you. God, you saved me, now use me."

Fully aware of the odds that were against me, and the taunts of the enemy saying that I would never make it, I walked out of that conference in tears. Without a doubt I knew that God had a plan for my life. Behind a car in the parking lot, I waited for Bobby. My heart was stirred with the call of God and so my tears flowed freely. As Bobby came out I approached him and told him what had happened to me that night.

Then unabashed, I told him that I wanted to be like him. "Please pray that I would pastor and pioneer one day." Bobby prayed and imparted an anointing for my life that night.

Setting My Heart on Chicago

Six years after I had been saved — I was coming to a place where I was maturing after allowing myself to be corrected and discipled — I was finally sent out to pastor. But not before facing some intense battles in my life.

Knowing that I was called to pastor, I chose Chicago as the city to pioneer a church. We were taught to announce it and then pray about it. Even Pastor was part of this process, for he too prayed about it. The waiting for me took four years. I fasted and prayed for Chicago, read up on it at the library and even wore a Chicago hat. Four years of waiting did not even dim my excitement about going there, but I had much to learn still. Certain things had to line up in my life.

It was coming up – the Praise Chapel Bible conference[7] where I would be sent off to pioneer. Because I worked the graveyard shift at that time, I was available to go to morning prayer and meet Pastor Neville at the church for coffee, sometimes even bringing him coffee. I loved it. There were times that the pastor had to send me home because he was busy. One day, I told him that I still wanted to go to Chicago.

"When do you feel like it will be God's timing?" I asked him.

He promised me that he would announce at the next Bible Conference that I would go to Chicago.

---

[7] Praise Chapel world conferences occurred every two years.

As far as I was concerned, I was ready. I made sure I had no debt. My car was used and paid for because I did not want to go into debt with car payments, and I chose not to own a credit card. I needed no strings to tie me to California when it was time to leave.

Several months before the conference, Pastor Neville met with Esther and me, "We have a situation," he began. "There will be a pastoral change for our church in Sacramento (California) and we need someone to take over. We want to give you a chance at it. We want you to pray about it." It was a fairly healthy church.

Esther and I agreed to pray. Two days later, we told him that after praying about it, we had no peace about it. And I still felt like I wanted to go far, to somewhere — like Chicago.

Pastor Neville agreed, "Okay, that's what we'll do."

Things changed overnight. I lost my job, and it was my best one I had at the time. Working for a dairy company making close to $18 an hour plus full benefits in 1993 was a great income. Being low in seniority though meant that when our company lost a big contract, nine of us lost our jobs.

"Okay, I can handle this." was my response. "God will provide."

"Hey, Kelly, I want you to pray about going to Redding, California." Pastor Neville said this a month later after he called my wife to meet with him at his office. No other details were given other than it was another pastoral change. "We need someone to go, someone who is willing. I wanted to run it by you and give you the first opportunity."

Esther and I prayed about it and we felt that we were not meant to do it. "Pastor I appreciate that but my heart is set on going to Chicago."

Pastor Neville was understanding "No problem," he replied "God will work it out. Just wanted to run it by you."

Wednesday night that week was the middle of a prayer revival, and I was asked to give a testimony. There was a large crowd and people were excited and fired up. Standing there sharing my testimony with everyone was an honor and so I relished that moment. I talked about how two years prior, someone stole my car and I lost my job about the same time. Eventually, I got my car back and I had a better job. I concluded then that no matter what, "the devil is a liar!" As I talked, I noticed an usher in the back waving his arms at me trying to get my attention. Being on stage at twenty-five years old was exciting and a big deal to me.

My thought was, *Forget that dude; this is my moment. I get to share my testimony.* Whatever that usher wanted, could wait.

As soon as I was off stage, that usher walked up to me and said, "Hey, bro, when you were on the stage testifying about them stealing your car, they just stole your car again, out of the church parking lot."

Unbelievable!

"What?"

He was sorry, "Yeah. We (he and the other ushers) feel real bad because it was a woman and she had a baby. When she put the baby in the car seat, we thought it was your wife. We actually waved goodbye to her. They drove off and then we went in to the church and we saw your wife teaching in the nursery, and we realized that we had made a mistake."

Now I was jobless and car-less again. Two weeks later we found my car completely stripped in the city of Compton, California. Why did it seem like whenever Pastor Neville offered me a church, something disruptive happened in my life?

The Curveball

Just two months away – that was how long it was before the long-awaited conference. Chicago was just around the corner. My excitement was growing. Also, Esther was pregnant and we were expecting our second child. It had been a month after the offer to Redding, California.

Pastor had another offer for me. "Hey, in Tacoma, Washington," I could tell where this was already going, "the pastor there is going to be doing something different. Would you be willing to go up there? We wanted to give you an opportunity. We know that you have plans we have scheduled for Chicago."

My heart was set with the reply, "Pastor, thank you but we have no peace about it. We just want to go to Chicago."

He said, "No problem."

We left it at that.

It was my wife's appointment with the doctor the next day. Since I had HMO insurance, Esther would see a different doctor for every visit. The wait was long so I went in search of coffee. When I returned with it, Esther was crying in the hallway in front of everyone in the waiting room.

Alarmed, I asked her, "What is going on?"

She said that the baby in her womb was dead! My baby! The doctor gave her the terrible news while I went to get coffee. According to the doctor, the baby's heart had stopped and it has been dead for a month. This was unimaginable!

We were confused, "We were just here a week ago and the doctor said that the baby was fine," we protested.

The doctor dismissed us after he advised, "Listen, if you want to come back in a week, we will give you a second opinion." Can you believe that?

Fair enough. We left still confused.

A week went by and our prayer was, "Oh Lord, please do something."

Even the church laid hands Esther and prayed. We clung to hope. But another ultrasound a week later confirmed that the baby was indeed dead.

The baby needed to be removed from her body. Immediately, they hooked up Esther to an IV and gave her medicine to induce labor. I was instructed by the doctor to stay with her. Watching my wife being sick from the medicine was hard. For eleven hours, she had cramps and was in severe pain. Then she asked me to help her to the bathroom. I waited for her outside the door.

A few minutes later, I heard Esther scream.

I opened the door and she was still sitting on the toilet, looking terrified. "Kelly," she said, "the baby came out in the toilet."

I ran to fetch the nurse.

The nurse came in, saw Esther sitting on the toilet and extremely upset, "What are you doing out of bed?" she scolded her. "You shouldn't be out of bed."

As calmly as I could, I explained to the nurse that the doctor gave me permission to help my wife to the bathroom (apparently, the nurses' strike that week was getting to this woman). My wife was in shock and still seated on the toilet seat.

"Well, I can't help you just sitting there!" the nurse snapped at my wife.

She grabbed Esther by the arm and I took the hint and helped her guide my wife back to the bed. Attached was the dead baby who was now dragging behind my wife as she struggled toward the bed. With Esther safely in bed, the nurse covered her with a blanket. But not after she took the dead baby and placed her between my wife's legs!

"Listen," she addressed Esther and me, "the hospital is very crowded and they put you on the wrong floor. The nurses are on strike this week. It will be about ten to fifteen minutes before I can get a doctor in here. You will be okay; just hang in there." She left and closed the door behind her.

There I was left in that room – with God, my wife, my dead baby, and the devil's taunting. Esther was weeping and I was just sitting there trying to comfort her. It is a day that I will never forget. In two months I was about to be sent out to pastor and everything seemed to be going wrong. The reality of my situation was almost disheartening.

Yet, I sat there and told God, "Lord, I just want to do your will."

I had been well discipled so that I understood that no matter what happened, God was going to see me through. Difficulties were not meant to move me. Doing the will of God was my focus – not my circumstances.

Finally, sometime later, the doctors came and did a D&C (dilation and curettage)[8] on Esther to remove the dead infant. Whatever they did wrong during that procedure resulted in my wife bleeding nonstop every day for six and a half years. But our hearts were still set on going out to pastor.

After being hospitalized for two days, Esther opted to go home (she had the option of staying an extra day there).

"No. Let's go do the will of God," she urged me. That woman was my hero! In the meantime, I got another job with a graveyard shift.

Six Long Years

Esther bled nonstop for six and a half years after that surgery. It seemed like we tried everything.

---

[8] A minor operation in which the cervix is expanded enough (dilatation) to permit the cervical canal and uterine lining to be scraped with a spoon-shaped instrument called a curette (curettage), www.medterms.com.

Not only was my wife spotting, she hemorrhaged blood. None of that hindered her from ministering and living life. She led worship and helped me with ministry. Though her bleeding was a challenge for us as a married couple, we weathered it. Doctors could not stop the bleeding. The longer it went, the more we saw our hope of having more children dissipate.

Early one morning, my son James (who was about six years old then) came over to my bed and woke me up.

"Dad, Mom is sleeping on the floor of the bathroom."

Half awake, I went to the bathroom to check on her and found that she was not asleep — she had passed out. That woke me up quickly. We took her to the hospital and discovered that she had lost more than half her blood. It is like a motor with half the oil, though it will run for a while, it will eventually stop. She could have died.

During that time, a pastor named Irvin Rutherford came to preach for us and he prayed for my wife. Her bleeding stopped. We were greatly relieved. My wife got back on a normal cycle, but we have never been able to have any more children.

****

How Much?

Multitudes followed Him. This man called the Christ was causing a stir wherever He went. They were drawn to Him because of the miracles and because of His love and compassion. While teaching them about the kingdom of God, He provided them with "free health care," and He fed them by multiplying fish and bread. No one else had done such things or shown such compassion. Suddenly, Jesus stopped and told them that if they did not drink His blood and eat His flesh and forsake all, they could not be His disciples. That crowd shrunk.

Then He turned and looked at Peter and His disciples and said, "Will you also leave?"

They replied, "We have forsaken all for you. We have nothing left. You have the words of life."

The gospel of today preaches that doing God's will is an easy thing. Nowhere do I find that in the Bible. Difficulties are equated with obeying God. Paul was doing God's will by going to a certain city but was stoned by those who opposed him (Acts 14:19; 21:32). Peter preached the gospel, but he was beaten and thrown in jail (Acts 5:18; 12:4,5). It was in God's divine plan for Jesus to go to the cross. Somehow we have attributed God's will as a place where there are no trials, testing and challenges. "Through many tribulations, we must enter the kingdom of God (Acts 14:22)."

Now that sums it up right there.

■■■

PART THREE

SEND ONE: THE PASTOR

CHAPTER ONE

The Road To Destiny

An Unexpected Switch

Then, the much-anticipated day of the conference came - the conference where Esther and I were to be released to pioneer a church in Chicago. It had been six years since I had waited for it.

"Kelly and Esther, to the city of Chicago!"

Our names were announced and there was the applause and the cheering from the audience, but for me, the excitement was not there. Everything that could have gone wrong went wrong. For years I had dreamt of that day and the excitement of finally being sent out. But as I walked up to the stage, hand in hand with my wife, I felt pretty beat up. The seeming road through hell in the previous three or four months prior to this conference had sucked the joy out of me. Add to that, I had to leave as soon as they were done praying for us because I had a night shift to work. My new job at the dairy made real good money. There was no time to savor the moment.

Three weeks after the conference, all the couples who were recently sent out met for a class. It was a prerequisite in preparation for leaving the mother church. Finally, this was the last step before we left for Chicago. But little did I know that God had a better plan that was about to unfold, a plan that would mess up mine. At that meeting, the assistant pastor asked to talk to me afterward. He had a message from Pastor Neville — pray about going to Kansas City.

Now, I loved Pastor Mike Neville for he was like a father figure to me, but not the assistant pastor. So for the assistant pastor to tell me to pray about going to another city instead of Chicago, well, I was not happy.

"Look man," my voice was stern, "every time you guys ask me to take a church, something bad happens to me. I'm going to Chicago, that's what God put on my heart," That was my final answer, or so I thought.

He looked at me as if he knew something I didn't, "Pastor really feels good about this. Why don't you just pray about it?"

I said I would but I did not really mean it.

On our way to the parking lot, Esther looked at me and stated, "You know, I really feel good about this." Not her too?

"Be quiet." I shushed her "I pray way more than you. We are going to Chicago."

Then very cocky, I reiterated as if repeating it would ensure our destination "We are going to Chicago."

The details of the church in Kansas City came to me a few days later. A pastor there was leaving a small pioneer work. Two families from the mother church in Huntington Park, the same church in California that I attended, needed a pastor. Two families were enough to start a church. Well, count me out. I was going to Chicago.

That Thursday night, I shared a message at a fellowship with the Bible study team leaders. I talked about sacrifices using the story of Abraham and Isaac. My point was, when we got saved, we gave up drugs, alcohol, cheating on our spouses and other such bad habits. After salvation, those were not really sacrifices any more, because we were used to them. God was always looking for a sacrifice from our life. Boy, did I eat my own words later!

One Way to Kansas City

Hands on my shoulders, Pastor Neville stopped and said, "Hey, boy," in that distinct country accent, "are you ready for Kansas City?"

This was Sunday night.

"I'm not going to Kansas City." I protested.

Like Dr. Spock, Pastor Neville squeezed my shoulder and affirmed, "Yes, you are!"

Right there, everything that I worked for, every trial, every teaching was on the line. Because I knew that when that man said that, I was going to do it.

Tears welled up in my eyes and I actually started to cry.

"Pastor, what about Chicago?" This was my last attempt.

"Kelly, if you really want to go to Chicago, you can go later. I have no one that wants to go that far to Kansas and we have two families there. I need you to do this."

By then, I understood that the Bible said that "shepherds" (or pastors) watch over our souls (Hebrews 13:17).

I replied, "Pastor, you will give an account. If you say this is God, I will go."

Without hesitating, he looked me in the eye and said, "It's God. I need you to go. You quit your job tomorrow and you leave Tuesday." And he walked away.

Wow! Talk about feeling like I just got ran over by a truck – a big truck!

I searched out the assistant pastor that night and said, "Dude, why didn't you tell me that he was going to make me?"

"I didn't want to tell you." he confessed. "I told you to pray about it and was hoping that God would speak to you."

But it was settled and just like that, my actual destination changed. No Chicago — I was to head for Kansas City, Missouri. Confused and filled with mixed emotions I went home. Being a pastor was great, but this change was abrupt and had not been on my radar. Thankfully, my brother-in-law, Carlos (he ended up going to pastor the church in Tacoma,

Washington), came over that night to my house, and I was glad for the company. It was good to have someone to talk to while taking in the news.

"Man, I'm going to do this, but..." My voice trailed off. I was still shocked and discouraged from the sudden change of plans.

Then I thought of an upcoming preaching appointment I had and said to Carlos "One of my best friends Ronnie Chavez...I was supposed to go preach for him but he hasn't called me." About right then, the phone rang. It was Ronnie.

"Dude, I was just saying your name." I exclaimed.

He said, "Well, there is a reason I'm calling. What is going on?"

Quickly, I began to tell him the recent situation. Thank God for Ronnie. He began to speak into my life, saying some key words that brought me peace, especially when he mentioned "obedience."

But God was not done confirming to me that He was in my change of destination. Early the next morning, which was Monday, my phone rang and woke me up. An old friend of mine when I first got saved was calling. This was the man who prayed for me to get filled with the Holy Spirit, but he was no longer a member of Praise Chapel. His call was out of the blue.

"Kelly," he revealed, "the Lord woke me up last night and told me to pray for you. The weirdest thing happened — I prayed all night and I could not sleep. I am at work right now and I wanted to call you when I got here." He continued, "This is what happened: I could not hear God's voice but I kept hearing your voice and you kept saying, 'When was the last time you sacrificed for God?'"

Those were my exact words at the Bible Study that I had taught last Thursday. He also proceeded to tell me that the Lord wanted me to lay down my Isaac to receive what He had for me. I knew what that meant. God wanted me to go to Kansas City.

Doing the right thing was important to me. And so was leaving the mother church the right way. Having settled in my heart that this move was God, I went in search of Pastor Neville early the next day, which was Monday. I told him that I was going to Kansas City the next day, and I was doing it with all my heart. We still had to finish packing. Come tomorrow, we would be on our way to Kansas City. Our farewell fellowship at my brother-in-law's house that night was quickly planned. Everyone came over to say goodbye.

Esther and I were leaving the house where it sort of all began for me – my grandpa's house with the garage apartment. This was the place where I surrendered my life to the Lord. It had been my home since I had been saved. This was also the house that Bobby, the mailman, had rented, as well as Albert. For a moment it appeared like it was going to be vacant again.

But Albert and Yolanda were back in California and needed a place to stay. They had returned to California the very week I was leaving for Kansas City, to help with the mother church. They had merged their church in Irving, Texas with his brother's church in Dallas, in order to make the move.

Calling up my grandfather, I said, "Listen, I am leaving, but Albert and Yolanda are here. Can they move back in the house?"

The answer was a definite yes.

Next door to grandpa's house lived a mean Catholic guy. He hated the Bible study meetings. Bobby was the first one who started having them in the house. He was greatly relieved (temporarily, of course) when Bobby moved out.

Clueless to the fact that Albert was also a Bible Study leader, he told Albert when Bobby was leaving, "Oh I'm so glad that they are gone. All that crazy stuff on Friday nights!"

He found that out soon enough.

When Albert left, that neighbor came over and told me, "Oh, I'm so glad, man, all that stuff, that 'toh toh toh toh' (mocking speaking in tongues)...I don't know what they are saying over there...but I'm glad they're gone."

Soon after, he discovered that I too led Bible Studies in the house and he began to persecute me. Occasionally, he had called the cops on our Bible Study group because we were singing.

As a farewell gesture, this neighbor came over to say goodbye with a bag of vegetables for my trip. He had known me since I was a kid.

"Wow, you guys are leaving!" He seemed happy and sad at the same time and it was hard to tell at first until Albert popped his head out of the truck and announced, "But I'm moving back!"

"Oh no!" He groaned. (Eventually, Albert and Yolanda purchased grandpa's house. For over thirty years, preachers have lived in that home).

Saying goodbye to family and friends was difficult. We were leaving everyone and everything that was familiar to us. That day, I parted with my best friend Abraham. We had been inseparable. We wept as we said goodbye.

"I want to bless you with something," Abraham said through his tears.

He gave me a picture of David and Goliath. The giant looked like he was fifty-feet tall with David holding a slingshot and appearing like an ant next to him.

Abraham's parting words were, "Dude, no matter what happens, don't quit!"

That picture remains one of my most cherished possessions because it had ministered to me in the tough times. It hangs in my church office today.

My mom did not take the news of our sudden move too well. To her, this was asking too much. She called Pastor Neville to let him know how upset she was about it.

"Aren't there enough sinners in California?" she grilled him. "He's my only child with my one grandson!" But that did not change anything.

With all our possessions loaded in the Ryder moving truck, I strapped my barbeque grill to the back of the truck, and we were ready to go. Just then, mom drove up to the house. When she saw me, she started screaming and crying.

Falling down weeping, she begged me, "Don't leave!"

It occurred to me then, my mom too had to pay the price for my doing the will of God. The reality of it all was settling in — I was really leaving. Esther's family was weeping as they said goodbye. We tore ourselves away from them and drove off – Esther and me, and our two year-old-son. In the rearview mirror, we watched them through our tears, standing there in the California sun, waving goodbye. Everything was happening so fast, it seemed like there was no time to think.

****

Obedience

I felt like Abraham when I went to Kansas City – clueless about the destination. My only assurance was that I was meant to go there. God's promise to Abraham was also for me.

"I will make you a great nation. I will bless you. I will make your name great. And you shall be a blessing."

My job was to go and God's part was to fulfill the rest of that promise.

Obedience to God's will brings a blessing. Abraham's life is evidence that obedience to God does not exempt us from setbacks or testing. Abraham had to contend with some major setbacks. His wife was barren even though God had promised him a son, he wandered around for a while, made mistakes (had Ishmael), got sidetracked, and had problems with his nephew, Lot, that caused him some difficulties in his ministry. He did not see the fruit of his obedience right away. Finally, when his promised son was a young man, God told Abraham to put him on the altar. He experienced much testing and probably an emotional roller coaster before he saw much of the promised blessing.

For believers today, we are the seed of Abraham. We carry the name of Jesus. His name is great and we become great because of what He has done for us. God promises that we will become a blessing. Ultimately, being obedient releases the blessing in our lives so we can bless others.

Within Abraham was this great potential and promise: "And in you, all the families of the earth will be blessed." Being the seed of Abraham through faith, we have this potential. What was in Abraham? It was not just his seed. It was his obedience. If he had never left his place of comfort, it would not have been a blessing to others.

Thus I thought about my decision when my pastor said, "You have to go."

What would have happened if I said to him, "God did not speak to me. You are controlling. This is not fair. This is not what I wanted. I know that you prayed but I did not pray about it. God did not show me this."

I could have said all those things to mark that moment. Everything I knew as a disciple was being tested. If I would have said any of those words or responded that way I wonder how many souls would not have been saved. Or how many lives we would not have impacted for God. Over the last eight years, we have performed a drama that we have led thousands of people to salvation.

I could have stopped all this if I had told my pastor "No, I want to do what I want to do."

I would have missed God. I did not know. I did not see many churches in the 1990s with over fifty people. If you had fifty people then, you were considered a mega church. In the early '90s, they found that 97 percent of churches in America had about fifty people.

I think now, *My God, what would have happened if I listened to my mom on that street telling me not to leave and coming against the man of God in my life?*

Those lives that I've seen turn to God would not have been changed.

****

CHAPTER TWO

Life as a Pioneer

Lost in Kansas City

I had never looked up Kansas City on a map let alone read up on it. Our excitement grew as our trip progressed. But the trip itself was not without its adventures and challenges. Not even two hours out of town to Barstow, our minivan got a flat tire. We were stuck overnight there to get that fixed. Then while driving through New Mexico, I hit a bump and my new minivan (someone had just given it to me) became unhooked from the moving truck. Hitching that bumper back up in the scorching desert heat was not easy. Esther had difficulty maneuvering that huge truck just right so I could attach the van to it. That took a long time. But we arrived safely in Kansas City, after traveling for about two days for about a total of thirty-some hours.

Kansas City was foreign to me. We had no idea what to expect. A family there was aware of our coming and had set up our reservations at the Drury Hotel. They also invited us over for dinner that first night and had us follow them to church for that first service. Our adventure in Kansas City had just begun.

The church met in an old historic church in downtown in Kansas City – a building that seated 900 people. In that huge building, a church of about seven people met for services. Two families made up the congregation plus a few other people that were coming. Preaching for the first time to those seven people was not hard, but seeing 893 empty seats was. Why was this small church meeting in this humungous building? This got more ridiculous because the next Sunday, the pastor who owned the building doubled the rent! For a small church to be paying the amount of rent it was, it made no sense at all.

After the first service I went to shake everyone's hand goodbye. Then they all left. It was only after they were all gone, that we realized we had no clue where we were. We had forgotten to make sure that we had directions back to the hotel. Figuring I might see a familiar landmark, Esther and I just started driving around.

"Do you know where we are?" I asked my wife. I could not even remember the name of the hotel. Thank God she did. But she too had no idea how to get there.

Then as we drove away, I remembered the offering.

"Are we supposed to get the offering?" Even as I asked Esther I knew the answer to that question. After all, I was the pastor and I needed the offering. Besides we had both seen someone place the offering behind the pulpit and no one else had touched it after that.

Since we were already driving in circles around the block, we decided to drive back to the church building. Another church was in the middle of their worship service when we arrived. I went around to the back of the stage where I could see the offering behind the pulpit.

"Oh, God, I gotta get that offering." I said to no one in particular, "but I don't want to make a bad impression."

Unsure of how to retrieve the offering basket without creating a disturbance, I turned to go and ran into a man wearing a dirty T-shirt, ripped-up Levis and sandals. He looked like he was painting or doing construction on the church.

"Sir," I asked, "can you help me out? I need to talk to the pastor."

He answered, "I am the pastor."

For a minute, I looked like a dummy.

I was apologetic, "Oh I'm sorry. I'm the pastor of the families that met here earlier. This is my first day, and I made a terrible mistake."

We were behind the stage and I pointed to the pulpit. "My offering basket is right behind there. Is there any chance you can get it?"

The man looked at me like "this guy does not know what he's doing." Retrieving the basket, he gave it to me.

"Thank you very much," I said and began to walk out the door.

This was September 11, 1993. Kansas City happens to be very windy about this time of the year – a fact that I learned later. Summer was about to end and give way to the fall. I took one step out the door and the wind blew the offering basket out of my hands, scattering the checks and the paper money all over the parking lot. Esther and I began to run after that strewn offering. We crawled under cars and chased after the offering while the wind toyed with it blowing it faster than we could run. Here was our first offering and we were about to lose it. The other pastor just stood there shaking his head as he watched us. He never offered to help. Certain that we had gathered the offering up from the parking lot, we had to figure out how to get back to our hotel. There was a visitor's card in the offering with his address and phone number and it was the only phone number we had of anyone in the area. It was worth a try. So I called him.

"Hey, I'm Pastor Kelly. You were here this morning. I got a situation. I don't know where I am at."

He gave me directions back to the hotel. This was truly a very humbling experience.

****

How Far Will You Follow?

Calculated risks. Career moves. Convenience. These are some of the reasons why some people would leave their place of comfort. Abraham's move was none of that. He did not know where he was going. All God told him was that God was going to show him the land. He did not really need to leave. The Lord just asked him to and Abraham obeyed. He did not really understand it.

I think about this scripture in light of my wife and me leaving our home and family to go pioneer a church in Kansas City. I felt like Abraham. All I had to do was to start moving and God was going to show me where I was to go.

"So then, none of you can be My disciple who does not give up all his own possessions (Luke 14:33)."

Other people have done much the same thing to accomplish a great purpose for God. They were called to leave their homes. People like John Knox, David Livingston and others who sacrificed all for God's call. These people left their families for long periods of time. But then Jesus did the same thing. He left heaven for earth where He became a servant on a sinful planet in a human body. That was not an easy call.

Leaving to go where God calls is a complete surrender to His leadings. This is not getting out of the boat while your hand is on the side of it in case it did not work out. Neither does that mean getting out of the boat to walk on the water, but you're wearing your life vest. It is getting out of the boat and taking a risk – you either sink or swim. That is radical, that type of punk rock mentality where you live on the edge, and I love it. It is putting all on the line and doing something crazy. Faith is not having a back up plan. Real faith is doing something that if it doesn't work, you can be in trouble.

We live in a day of GPS. It will tell you when to turn and plan out the path for you. Sometimes we live our lives with God that way. But God does not show us the planned directions all at once. In God's economy, taking a risk for the Lord has its rewards.

"And everyone who has left houses or brothers or sisters or father or mother or children or farms for My name's sake, will receive many times as much and will inherit eternal life (Matthew 19:29)."

He was talking about leaving some of our most committed relationships for the sake of the gospel. When we are trying to fulfill the call of God, we can look forward to our heavenly reward. Consider the fact that we cannot look to be paid now in this lifetime. The decisions we make now will determine how we live forever.

■■■

Home Not So Sweet Home

We lived in that hotel for about a week. Moving my family out of there and into a house was my first priority. This was unfamiliar territory for me. Everything looked different, the terrain and the houses included. I started scouring the newspapers for houses to rent.

Dusk was falling when I met a realtor in front of a house. The house and yard looked huge. What a screaming deal, I thought – for that size of a house! Homes in the Los Angeles area where I lived were smaller and closer together with the yards consisting of a few feet of grass. But looks can be deceiving. After I moved into the house, I learned a major lesson – never rent a house in the dark.

Soon after, I moved the church meeting to my living room. Our current church rent was outrageous for the number of people we had. The house I rented was hardly a better deal when I discovered that the only good thing about it was the fresh paint. I had made the deal out of desperation and ignorance about what to look for when renting a home. And we were stuck in it for a while.

Winter was fast approaching when we discovered some major flaws with the house. During the first freeze, I went to take a shower and realized that the pipes were frozen. For eleven days, we had to take showers at other people's houses. In order to keep the pipes from freezing again, I had to leave the water running. Cracks in the front of the house let the winter air blow in so that the house was always cold.

Every moment I was home during the cold months, I kept feeding wood to the wood stove. I stayed close to that fire reading my Bible and staring at it, because I was so cold.

Then one day, while I was in the house I heard a crashing noise in the garage. Esther had gone to the garage to get something. By the time I got to the garage, she was drenched in water and covered with sheet rock. The pipes in the ceiling had defrosted and burst and the sheet rock on the ceiling fell right onto her.

I thought, *Oh my God, what kind of place is this?*

The house was not the only thing that presented us with problems – our neighbors did. The house was on a semi-commercial street and we had two neighbors. One Saturday, our family took about a twenty- to thirty-minute trip down the road to get some food. We went to Kentucky Fried Chicken to pick up a meal and then stopped at the Perkins restaurant to buy a pie. Upon returning home, we found that the front door was cracked open.

I mumbled to myself, "I thought I shut this door."

After making my plate, I sat down on my couch to eat. Saturday meant football so I leaned over to turn on the television and realized that it wasn't there anymore. Then I saw that even the VCR was gone. We had been robbed, completely cleaned out of anything of value. Our checkbooks had also been swiped, both our personal one and the church's. We suspected the thief was someone who knew our comings and goings. One of our neighbors was having a party and we knew that they had drugs there. But they were of no help. They ducked inside their house as soon as they saw me come out.

Days later, we began to receive thousands of dollars of bad checks, even from other states. Whoever stole our checkbook must have sent if off to some friends or took a long road trip. Checks were written at the nearby mall and places in Dallas, Texas and in Denver, Colorado. Even after we closed the account, the mess continued. It seemed like it would never end. But I had been there before. I had been robbed and carjacked in the past so I was not shaken up.

For our first Christmas (we moved there in September), my mother and my grandma blessed us with gifts that amounted to about $700. Both had giving hearts and missed us tremendously. It was their way of expressing their love and care for us. We eagerly awaited the arrival of the huge care package by UPS. Money was scarce when we pioneered. But the package took a long time to arrive and my mom kept calling to see if we got the box. No such delivery. A few days before Christmas, mom got concerned and traced the package. She was told that the package got delivered and someone signed for it. We were sure it wasn't us. And I had my suspicions.

"What kind of things and toys were in that box?" I asked my mom on the phone.

With each description, my suspicions were confirmed. Each item was identical to my neighbor's new stuff, from the new jacket the neighbor was wearing, to his kids' brand-new toys. UPS washed their hands clean of the situation. They said that they could not do anything because there was no way to prove that my neighbor stole my care package. So our Christmas that year was bare.

Well, at least we had a Christmas tree! A few days before Christmas, I sat in the living room in front of the wood-burning stove staring at the fire. It had been a crazy few months, but we were in it for the long haul.

Suddenly, my wife screamed and pointed at the Christmas tree. "There is something in the tree!" she cried.

Apparently, we weren't the only tenants in that house. Two huge rats were in the Christmas tree.

I shooed them out while thinking, *What kind of house did I pick?*

But our church continued to meet there, out of necessity.

This Is No Los Angeles!

Our small church was struggling in that house. Efforts at outreaches and witnessing yielded little. For our first visitor's Sunday, one person brought someone from work – and the visitor never came back. The few families we had did not invite many people to our small church. Breakthroughs came, but they were slow.

It started when Pete Woody absentmindedly drove past my house one Sunday morning. Pete was a little slow on some things. That particular Sunday, he forgot where to turn and went past my house. He had driven to my house for a few Sundays but somehow that Sunday he whizzed right on by. Pete's mistake ended up being a God-led one.

Walking in late, Pete commented, "Pastor, I spaced out and drove past your house. Do you know there is a church down the street that is empty?"

"What are you talking about?" I asked.

Now I am a creature of habit. I had never driven past my house in the other direction. There was never a need to drive that far, for the grocery store and the freeway were to my left when I drove out of my driveway. Whatever was to my right, I had not bothered to find out, until that day.

After our service, we all went down the street to check out Pete's story. Sure enough there was a church building there, but it was not empty. It was a Seventh Day Adventist church and they met on Saturdays. The following week, I went to inquire about sharing their building. A definite yes! They were actually looking for somebody to share it with. Moving into this building was exciting, and it was our first one. Finally, we could have our first revival and outreach.

Don Macamish was the first evangelist we invited to preach at our new location. Back then it was a common practice to put a picture of the evangelist and his name on the flyer. Then we would add a catchy phrase like "Come expecting God to move" or "Come expecting a miracle." We lived within walking distance of the Super Walmart or Hyper Mart that was by the mall. Generally, there were about eight hundred to a thousand cars there twenty-four hours a day. David Barbosa, (the husband of the first family that came to my church whose wife Connie has been my administrative assistant now for eleven years) made it a practice of coming over to my house for prayer every day and then we would meet after his work to go outreach.

It was there that I got introduced to obvious prejudice.

Glancing at the picture on the flyer I just gave her, the black woman remarked, "I'm not going to no whitey church!" Then, wadding it up, she tossed it away.

That was a culture shock that shook me to the core. This was not Los Angeles – a multicultural city where I was somewhat a minority. This was Kansas City, Missouri. Chalk that up as a new revelation. Certainly, I was not naive to racism. All my life, I had lived and attended schools where all my friends were from different nationalities and backgrounds. Even in my church I was in the minority – but the thought never crossed my mind that it was a problem. After that incident, I began to notice a trend. If the picture on the flyer was that of a black evangelist, only black people came. If it was that of a white man, we only had white visitors. After a while, I stopped putting pictures on the flyer.

Claiming to be saved was another discovery. It seemed like most of the people that I talked to profess to be Christians. At the projects and the apartment complexes, I ran into people who went to church or sang in the choir but they were drunk or smoking crack. Some of them sang in the choir, but they were cussing. Once in a restaurant, a pastor who was drinking at the bar heard me talking and invited me to drink with him. I couldn't believe it! That was a rude awakening. I was dumbfounded by their claims and their lifestyles that contradicted the claims.

I thought to myself, *Wow, everyone thinks they are saved here!*

What a sharp contrast to Los Angeles! At least in Los Angeles, when I witnessed to people on the street, they knew they were not saved.

And they said so. "Yeah I know I'm going to hell and I don't care."

These were different mentalities. In Kansas City, people seemed highly aware of race and thought that they were all saved.

Outreach after outreach, nothing would transpire.

"Pastor, when do you think people will start coming?" David asked me one night as we sat in front of Walmart witnessing to people. There was a lull in the stream of people coming in and out of the store. David was so loyal and faithful.

"David, I really don't know. All I know is that God told me to come here. Noah preached for all those years and no one listened. The bible says that one plants, one waters and God gives the increase. All I know is that if the rapture happened, I would rather be out witnessing and not sitting on my couch doing nothing."

But we did not give up. We planned a New Year's Eve service. The lineup included a drama, skits and food. We expected the neighborhood to come. But we had only two visitors for that service, a sixteen year-old girl and her boyfriend. Her name was Pamela.

She was so pregnant that when I asked her, "When is your baby due?" she replied, "Tonight."

Her due date was that night. Later, I found out the only reason she came was so her boyfriend would not go out to party with his friends.

"We are going to church" she told him and dragged him there.

Everything that night, the drama, the testifying and preaching were pointed to these two people. Both responded to the altar call. In one year, we got one soul saved.

They were a rough couple who needed a lot of help.

"Okay, God, we are going to go for it," I said to the Lord.

Pamela lived a couple of blocks from me. Her boyfriend was with me when I went to do a follow-up. That ended up being a most interesting visit. When we walked into the house, Pamela's mother was drunk and beating the tar out of Pamela's sister with a belt buckle. The woman was in a screaming rage. She then turned and started beating on pregnant Pamela.

She was yelling while I stood there praying, "Oh, Jesus!"

In her rage, she turned to me and asked, "Do you want some too, Preacher?"

"No, no." I replied.

Eventually, we got Pamela out of her mom's house and she had her baby. Due to her bad situation, Esther and I let her move in with us. Later she stayed with David and Connie Barbosa. We were trying to build a church and help people. And many of them were needy.

Not long afterward, we moved out of that terrible house into a duplex.

Fulfilled Vision

The unforgettable moment was surreal. It was also monumental in my life. Abraham, my friend, was jumping around preaching a revival. People were worshipping, and dancing with some falling out on the Holy Spirit. Suddenly, God reminded me of the vision he gave me six years earlier.

This was the exact moment I saw years before. There I was in the front pew wearing a suit. And Abraham, my friend, was preaching a revival. Pastor Neville had just officially made Abraham an evangelist. I was the pastor of this church. This was the building. This was the time. Tears began to flow down my face.

I felt the Spirit of the Lord come upon me and He said, "I told you so."

All my concerns as a new pastor that night were put at ease. There were times that we were nervous and unsure that we had made the right decision by pioneering in Kansas City. After all, we had left our familiar surroundings and family and, so far, we had seen no fruit. The ground was hard. But that night, the peace of God came upon me and I knew that I had made the right decision. God's assurance that night when Abraham was preaching carried me through many hard times later.

God was so faithful to His words. I learned then to never write off a new convert if they say that God wants them to do this or that — because we never know.

****

One Prayer, One Life to Give

It reminded me of what happened to Saul and his conversion. In Acts 9, Paul was harassing the church and was on his way with a letter authorizing him to persecute Christians. But he had a radical conversion. With one prayer, Paul's life was changed. That was like mine. I prayed one prayer and was radically transformed. It did not take me six months to be converted.

God attached Paul to someone who would care for him. God sent him Ananias. This man of God was scared of Saul (it reminded me of Albert's initial apprehension about me). But God had to assure Ananias that He had his hand on Saul to bring many to the Lord.

Moments after Saul's conversion, God spoke to Ananias that He had chosen and called Saul to be a preacher and a minister of the Gospel. Right after his conversion, he was called to be a preacher. It was not a long, drawn out process for years. Then we are humbled like little children and excited about God's plan for his life, when God can speak to us the best. Right then at the beginning, we are open and God can tell us what he wants us to be. Just like me. God showed me something that challenged me right at the beginning. Can you imagine a man who was murdering Christians but now told by God that He was going to use him to reach the Gentiles? The Jews were not even reaching the Gentiles. The Gentiles were the people you did not want in your church if you were a Jew.

God showed Paul that he was going to suffer much doing God's will (Acts 9:16). You know why God sometimes does not show us His call and all that we are going to do for Him? We probably would not do it if we realized all the testing and all the stuff we have to suffer through. Even if God showed us the good stuff, we might be blown away and not believe him!

It was not until many years later that Paul began to fulfill it. He had to go through a lot during that process to fulfill that word.

****

CHAPTER THREE

The Other Kansas City

Floating Flyer with Footprints

J-O-B. I needed one. As a pastor with a small congregation, my second priority in Kansas City was to find a job. My trucker's license allowed me to drive a vehicle carrying hazardous materials, so I got a job as a local propane deliverer. The map was my constant companion for that first month, although I was lost about half of the time. My long hours were exhausting and I stank – literally. Propane stinks like rotten eggs. Sometimes there was no time to get out of my work clothes so I went to church smelling like rotten eggs.

Pioneering was not easy.

"God, this is hard stuff," I complained to God.

It was my second winter and I had never driven in snow, and my job required that I drive in it all day.

We had been at the Missouri side in the Seventh Day Adventist building for a year and we had seen only one salvation.

After a month or two of outreaching, a tall, big Indian guy came into the church. He was holding a flyer with footprints on it that he found on the ground.

When I greeted him at the door, he asked, "Is this, this church?" He pointed at the flyer.

"Yeah! Come on in."

How he found it was a mystery to me. We had no sign outside (we could not have one) to indicate our church, though there was a Seventh Day Adventist sign. Since he was the first visitor in a long time, he became the focus of all the attention. There was plenty of food and so we fed him as he told me his story.

He attended another church in Lee Summit, Missouri, which was about twenty minutes away from our church. His job was to deliver newspapers to the nearby Walmart, and his schedule and paper route usually did not allow him to get back in time for services. One of our flyers was floating around in the parking lot when he saw it. Finally, he asked if he could come to our church periodically if he did not make it back to his.

I said, "Absolutely."

Our church was hosting the Praise Chapel from Dallas group, who performed a drama called, *Homie, Don't you know me*? It was a story about gangs. As the pastor, I went up and shared my testimony and our vision to reach those on the streets and everybody. The visitor was blown away by my testimony.

A week later, he was back with news. "Pastor Kelly," he said, "I met with my Pastor this week and I told him about you and he was excited and blown away about it."

"Really?"

"Yeah. My Pastor's got a radio show and he would really like you to come on the radio show with him."

"That is great!"

But in my mind I was thinking of all the reasons why I could not go on that radio show. I just started a full time job with no possibilities of getting off work in the middle of the day. The radio station was about forty-five minutes into Kansas City, Kansas (though it broadcasted everywhere), and no one in our fellowship did radio ministry at the time. It would be a paradigm shift. I was not really interested in the offer.

But every week, the Indian man pestered me about it.

"My pastor wants to know why you haven't called him. He really wants you to come on. He has a heart for reaching the people on the street and he is doing a series on it. He is really going to be blessed. I told him that you were a punk rocker and now you are a pastor."

But I kept blowing him off. Finally, the pastor got a hold of my phone number.

He called and said, "Hey, man, Paul told me about you and I would really like you to come on the radio show."

Happy and flattered that he considered me, I still tried to squeeze out of it. "I don't know if I can get off work," I said.

But he insisted, "Check it out because we would love to have you on our show this Friday."

Getting permission from my boss was not easy. Although he was reluctant and unhappy about it, he let me go. "Okay, you can go on your lunch break and stay, but you need to get out here early for your next shift."

That Friday, I traveled to the radio station and met Pastor Larry Stacey. Being on the air was exciting. We were both enthusiastic sharing and talking on the air and there was a good flow to our conversation. Larry was excited to hear my testimony of how God touched my life and how I wanted to reach the lost, and I was more than happy to tell it. People were calling in.

At the end of the show, Pastor Stacey said, "We have had a blessed time today and don't forget to tune in again next week because Pastor Kelly is going to be here with us again."

My heart sunk, "Oh God," I thought, "I'm going to be fired!"

But I went and asked again for time off to do the radio show. "You know I'm a pastor," I reminded my boss. Again, he reluctantly gave me the time off to go.

Three weeks later, the manager of the radio station called to see if I could meet with him. We met one day after work. It was the KCNW 1380 AM radio station and it was the only Spirit-filled charismatic-type station with a more upbeat feel.

The manager, Nick Marchi, said, "Pastor Lohrke, I actually heard you on Pastor Stacey's show the last couple of weeks." He added, "I'm telling you right now, I was blown away by your testimony."

He continued talking "I've been praying about something. I've been praying about doing something really different here. I want to reach people. I look at this as a ministry. I really feel that God brought you here for a reason. My idea is that, I want you to do a live radio show so that it is not typical preaching, but you come in and you play Christian punk rock and rap."

This was 1994. It was unheard of to play those types of music in church.

"I want to reach these young people. I really feel good about it. You can do whatever you want. You can talk right into that mike and be yourself. We will do a live call in." Then he made an offer "I will let you have this radio show for $50 for half an hour." This was a screaming deal to do a radio show.

Right away I was hesitant. "I don't know," I said. "I work and I don't know if I am able to do this."

His enthusiasm, however, was getting to me. "We are going to promote this in the Christian bookstores, and we are going to get flyers out to other churches and youth groups. I really feel like this is going to take off." Seeing I was not sold on the idea, he upped his offer. "As a matter of fact, I'll give you one hour for fifty bucks!"

I was floored, "Wow!" But in my mind I was thinking, *I'm Praise Chapel. We don't do radio.*" Never had I seen it done before and I didn't think it was something I would do.

Then I said what I thought any new pastor might say, "I'll pray about it."

As I'm walking out the door, he said, "Stop! I really feel this is good. Two hours for fifty bucks! This is going to take off. I know this is God." Amazing! The offer seemed to get better the longer I was there. But I would not commit.

I left. Back then when I was pioneering, I was inexperienced. By saying that I was going to pray about it, that really meant I was going to call my Pastor and ask what he thought.

As soon as I got home, I contacted Pastor Neville, "Hey, Pastor, guess what happened to me today?" Then I proceeded to tell him about the radio show and the offer.

He asked, "Kelly, what did you tell him?" he asked.

"I said, "I'll pray about it."

"No, you dummy! This is your breakthrough! You call him back and tell him that you are going to take it. You get on the radio. This is your open door. We are doing this!" After that phone call, I called the radio manager and told him that I accepted his offer.

Thus began my show called *Fired Up With PK* (Pastor Kelly). This was before the Promise Keepers was even known. It was a crazy time, but I loved it. There I was talking live and playing hardcore

Christian music late at night. We were doing crazy skits just to reach people.

"If you are out there driving," I would say on the air, "and you are messed up, loaded, I want you to call in. If you tuned in to this station by accident," we were just going for it, "come here right now and we'll pray for you." People actually drove in to the station for prayer and we would pray for them. This thing got crazy.

Within a few months, I stopped paying and they gave me the radio time slot for free. Soon I was hired to do the radio show for five hours instead of two! And it became the most popular show in that whole radio era. We averaged about sixty calls a night. All ages and kinds of people called in to the program. Some were kids having problems with their parents, kids who were suicidal, adults with problems and the occasional harassments. There were Satanists who called just to harass us. But we kept on preaching, doing crazy stuff and playing music.

One Bold Move

The radio ministry was exploding but the church was not. Although we were having a great time, there was no breakthrough – it was enough to discourage me.

So I said, "Lord, we need to move."

Our current location in the Seventh Day Adventist church building hid us from the public. We needed to be seen, to be out there, so checking out buildings was our next step. The first one we found did not work out. We were shut down because the owners did not want a church there. Another building looked promising. Late one night, some of the guys and I went and marched around that building seven times. Some of us were laying hands on the building and praying when a cop drove up.

With both hands on the building, that must have been an odd sight in the middle of the night. We must have looked like we were ready to be arrested.

"What are you doing?" the cop demanded.

While trying to explain to him that we were praying and believing for the building, here came two of the guys around the corner screaming and singing, "In the name of Jesus, in the name of Jesus, we have the victory..."

The cop said, "You guys are crazy! Get out of here!"

That building did not work out. We found one later.

Located in downtown Kansas City, this Hallmark building was perfect. It was in an open area. We were excited. The Seventh Day Adventist church received our two-week notice immediately. They were able to find another church to share their building with them right away. In the meantime, we spun our vision of what we wanted to do with our new building. The deal was sealed – until the inspection. It was a week before we were going to move in and the fire marshal and the realtor were there checking out the building. Their approval was necessary before we could rent the place. Suddenly, the fire marshal looked up into the rafters and saw evidence of a past fire. The building was condemned.

He concluded, "No one can be in this building. In fact it needs to be torn down."

Oh my God, I don't have a building! was my first thought. *I can't go back to the one I had.*

There was a rush of memory — how I had talked the big faith talk to my church and how the five buildings we attempted to rent amounted to nothing.

Discouraged, I went home that night crying.

"Babe," I mourned to my wife, "I've been here for a year and nothing seems to be going right. It has been so difficult. I know I got this radio show, but I did not come here to be a D.J. I came here to pioneer a church. No one is getting saved in the church."

Then I got mad. Always a man who feared God, something was different that night. My prayer was bold and specific.

I cried as I prayed, "God, I can't take this." Then with my fist in the air, I said to the Lord, "You have twenty-four hours to speak to me. I need to know something. Twenty-four hours, God!"

My wife, whose arm was around me as I prayed, grabbed my hand and said, "Oh, honey, don't talk to God that way."

Snow and sleet were coming down hard the next day as I drove home from work. Driving on the icy roads was difficult, especially since I was not familiar with it. My minivan was driving on Interstate 470 that went over Interstate 71 when it hit a pothole. The van slid and I lost control. I saw the wall coming up fast and knew that the freeway below was waiting. Everything was happening in slow motion.

Within those split seconds, my mind was working furiously. I was dead meat. God was going to kill me for yelling at him yesterday. Esther was going to remarry and someone else was going to raise my kid.

Just before my van kissed the wall, I screamed, "Jesus!" Then my head hit the windshield and darkness took me.

A tap on my window woke me.

"Are you okay?" It was a tow truck driver.

He was the first one to find me and he offered to tow my vehicle. My van was totaled.

The ambulance arrived soon after and I was loaded me onto a gurney. The paramedics rolled me toward the ambulance when it dawned on me — I was a man without a car or health insurance. This could end up costing me a bundle of money that I did not have.

Hardly able to think clearly because I was all banged up (I could not move my neck and excruciating pain was going up my back), I mumbled, "How much is this going to cost?"

"Sir, don't worry about that, you are hurt," one of the paramedics said.

But I persisted "Look, I need to know how much this is going to cost." A police officer was there and I made sure he heard me. "I'm not getting in this ambulance until I know how much it costs."

"Well, just to go to the hospital, it is about $450," the paramedic replied.

"I have no insurance," I explained. "I can't go to the hospital. I will be okay."

To clear themselves of all responsibilities relating to any of my injuries, the paramedics had me sign a paper. But I needed a ride home. The policeman agreed to give me one after I told him that I was a Christian. (Eleven months later, I finally got another vehicle).

The car accident had injured my back. While lying at home on the couch in pain, a brother from the radio station came over and prayed for me. My back got totally healed. It was a miracle.

But I still had no car and no church building. That next week I had to do my radio show and it was right before Christmas. The sales people, disc jockeys, manager and other employees were having a Christmas party in the basement. For the first time, I saw the basement. It was a pretty nice.

The manager of the radio station Nick and his wife Linda came to me and said, "Pastor Kelly, we heard about all that you have been going through and we feel so bad. We really believe in what God is doing in your life and in your ministry. We know that you don't have a building and you don't even have a car right now."

Then he suggested, "Why don't you move your church here to the radio station?"

Right then, I was thinking, a church in a radio station? No way. This messed with my paradigms.

I said, "We are forty-five minutes away from here. How much are you going to charge me?"

"You don't understand," Nick insisted. "I want to bless you. Just move in. You bring your church here, and you pay no rent. I just want you to come here. We would be honored to have you."

I prayed about the offer and decided it was God's will. Our church moved to the radio station. Surprisingly, most of the people in the church lived halfway between the radio station and the old church building.

We had officially left Kansas City, Missouri, for Kansas City, Kansas.

Church in the Radio Basement

Carpeted with a small stage, the basement worked for our church at the time. With concrete walls, the ceiling was open so that when the toilet upstairs was flushed, it was heard clearly downstairs. Also, when the air conditioning was on, water from it dripped down onto one of the rows. But we managed to over-look those small problems. This was our church. We added another bathroom downstairs and used one of the storage rooms as a classroom. It was home to our church for two years.

The difference in responses to our outreaches was noticeable. Our first outreach in Kansas City, Kansas, had a better response than we ever had in Kansas City, Missouri (that is nothing against the Missouri side). People in Kansas were open, readily accepted the gospel, and our church began to grow. Finally, I felt like this was where I needed to be. It seemed like God got me back on track.

Giving directions to my church on the air during my radio show was easy – we were located at the station. People started coming. The radio station was gracious and promoted our ministry. Any call to the station for prayer was forwarded downstairs to our church. I literally built my church on this response. We were having a tremendous time there and we experienced such freedom as a church at the radio station.

Perhaps the most memorable phone call that was ever forwarded to me happened in the middle of the day. A young girl called asking for help. She said that she was on a bus with satanic cult members (satanists) and they had traveled from New York. The girl wanted to be free from the cult but was afraid that they were going to get her. She sounded terrified. Her situation seemed unreal, almost like something you would hear or see on a movie.

While taking the call, I did not believe her at first. Was she exaggerating? Was this a prank? I was not sure. Finally, I told her that if she was serious about being free then she should meet me at the Bethany Hotel.

To check out her story, I took Steve (he is now one of my assistant pastors) with me, plus my wife and young son. Steve was single and living with my family at the time. After telling everyone to wait for me, I went into the hotel to find this girl – if she was even for real. I was looking for a sixteen-year-old girl but I did not see one except a woman of about forty sitting there. Certain that I had been fooled by a prank phone caller, I began to walk out of the hotel.

Just then, the Holy Spirit said, "You walked right past her."

Well, it couldn't be. But this was God directing me.

So I walked back, looked at this woman and asked, "Are you waiting for me—Pastor Kelly?"

She lifted up her head to look at me, and this supposedly sixteen-year-old girl appeared old and rigid. Too old, I thought. But she nodded. Dressed in black, the girl's face was pale and her eyes were sunken in making her appear older than her actual age.

She started crying "I'm scared they are going to get me if I get in the car."

I said, "Who is going to get you?"

She pointed across the street to some men loitering there. Somehow, I got her to get into my car and we drove off. We put on worship music and all of a sudden this girl in the back seat started growling and vomiting. She appeared to be demon-possessed.

My son was in the back seat and was crying, "Dad!"

All of a sudden, the transmission got stuck in low gear. And we drove slowly all the way to church. Something was not right. Once we got to church, we set her in the back row. That being a Wednesday night, we had service, and worship had already begun. At that time, we used worship CDs. As soon as this girl walked into the building, all the power went off. We could not worship. The worst part was that she was sitting in the back row and she was manifesting.

Not to freak out our visitors and kids, I told Esther to take another woman with her and this girl to another room and to pray for her. The minute the girl left, the sound system came back on. Coincidence? I did not think so. God's presence was there during the worship, but halfway through it, the Lord impressed on me to go and check on this girl.

What I saw when I opened the door was the most bizarre thing I had ever seen. The girl was fully manifesting and was flinging my wife and the other woman across the room like they were rag dolls. Her skin was pasty white and her throat was swollen up into a ball that looked like a goiter. She was drooling green vomit. The white of her eyes was blood red. I had to literally jump on her to hold her down and even then, I could barely do it. This was the sort of thing that you saw in the movies, never in real life, I thought, but I was proven wrong that day.

I began to rebuke the demon. Her mouth opened and a voice came out of it, but her tongue was not moving. It was talking to me in a horrible screech. The voice said that her mother was a satanist and she had given her up as a baby to this satanist group.

It screeched, "She was dedicated on my altar. She belongs to me!"

I began to pray.

Then I spoke directly to the girl. "Listen, say this prayer to renounce this curse on your family."

As we began to pray, there was a sound of fingernails scratching a chalkboard, but we ignored it and finished praying. All of a sudden, it stopped. Right in front of my eyes, the girl's skin became blush and the white returned to her eyes. She turned back to a sixteen-year-old girl.

You can just imagine how excited I was to preach that night. I had just seen a girl set free from demonic oppression. Exhausted from what she had been through, the girl just sat peacefully in the back row. We had a time of prayer and ministry to people during the altar call. During the ministry time, the girl asked my wife who the tall men were that stood on the stage, with robes on that said, "Righteousness, Holiness and Peace." They had swords in their hands. I was the only one on the stage. The girl was seeing angels.

Later, we sent the girl off to her family. She was completely free.

Divine Connection

It was a Sunday morning and I was going to church – in the radio station basement.

Noticing that Nick the manager of the radio station was working, I stopped.

"Hey, Nick, how are you doing?" I called. "Do you have to work on Sunday?"

"Yeah. Somebody called in."

It dawned on me that I had this working relationship with Nick and yet I did not know about his personal life.

"Where do you go to church?" I asked.

"I don't go anywhere."

"What? We are here doing all this ministry and you're..." My voice trailed off and then I asked, "What happened?"

He told me his story. The pastor of the church he attended had a moral failure and that hurt him and his wife. After that, they had a hard time trusting.

I tried to encourage him, "Bro, you gotta trust God again. You gotta do what's right Nick and bring your family." At the same time, I was fully aware that this was my landlord who gave me free rent. "I'm not saying that to get you to come to my church. But you need to go somewhere. God has a plan for your life."

Two weeks later, he showed up in church with his wife, Linda. His daughter, Lisa, and son-in-law, Eddie Forshey, a young married couple, started coming to church too. They too had stopped going because Nick used to be their youth pastor.

Today, Lisa, the daughter of that radio station manager, is one of my full-time administration assistants. Eddie, her husband, flourished in business and has traveled with me all over the world. Later, he built a beautiful house in which I live for free, and he will also be building our new church facility for free.

All this came about because we started with passing out flyers.

For two years our church met in that basement. We had grown to the point where we needed more room. It was time to move. Just four miles down the road in Kansas City, Kansas, we found an empty grocery store that became the new location for our church. It was a step of faith for us because for the first time in two years, we had to pay rent. The four-thousand-square-foot building was perfect. When we had our services there, we began to have revival and we grew again. Families started coming and we saw many lives beginning to change.

CHAPTER FOUR

Moments in the Spotlight

Rousing Barnes and Noble

Not long after that, I got on television unexpectedly.

Focus on the Family[9] was airing a program about a controversy over child pornography books from France. The dispute was over whether these books were child pornography or not. My wife who was listening to this story was intrigued by the debate and decided to take her ladies' Thursday morning prayer group down to the nearest Barnes and Noble.

The books showed photos of naked children, boys and girls, from ages five to seventeen showing their genitals. Some of the photos included adults with the children in inappropriate positions. One disturbing

---

[9] An American Christian ministry, founded by James Dobson, that nurtures, protects and defends family values worldwide.

picture was that of a twelve-year-old girl posing on a cross as Jesus, with full frontal nudity. This was under the guise of photo art. But they were pretty disgusting. There was no doubt in Esther's mind and those of the women with her that the books were child pornography.

Esther called the police and then me. I drove down to meet her in the store. The police showed up full stock and barrel to investigate. Denying any knowledge of the offensive books, the store manager claimed that it was impossible for him to read every single one. After all, there are thousands of books that are sold in his store! But he was very cooperative. Without further ado, the police confiscated the cases of books.

Afterward, the sergeant asked me, "Pastor Lohrke, is there anything we can do? Are you satisfied with this response?"

Still stunned at how these books came to the store in the first place, I replied, "Yeah, what about the other Barnes and Nobles?" There were two other Barnes and Nobles in our area, across the border in Missouri, within the three adjacent counties.

The manager assured me that the books would be removed from those two Barnes and Nobles too. He said not to worry about them, and until the District Attorney figured out the whole situation, the books would be kept off the shelves. Fair enough. But I was not convinced.

Two brothers from the church went with me the next day to check out the other Barnes and Nobles. We wanted to make sure that they had removed the books. We had our doubts. Sure enough, the main Barnes and Nobles in the Plaza in Missouri still had them out on the shelf for sale. We took a whole stack of them and laid them out on the table before we asked for the manager. She came and saw me and then looked at the book I had. Her expression showed that she was expecting it.

"I'm Pastor Kelly." I introduced myself, "I don't know if you have heard of what happened down at the Barnes and Noble in Leawood, Kansas, at your other store."

"Yeah, I heard about you," she snapped, "There is something called freedom of speech."

"Well, I understand that" I said. "But this is child pornography!"

"That is your opinion." She was very defensive.

"Well, these are not drawings" I explained. "These are photographs. These are actual kids."

I had enough common sense before to research the Federal Penal Code on child pornography, which states any child photographed or filmed underage with their genitals showing is deemed child pornography.

The lady fired back, "This is art. I would even have my daughter look at it. It does not even bother me."

"Here is the problem I have with what you are saying," I said. "If I rip a page out of your book, make photocopies and go out in front of your store and hand them out, I will go to jail. But you are saying to me that if people spend their money here, you would consider it art? This is not art."

"I don't care what you are saying!" the woman responded. She was adamant and even called me a right-wing fanatic.

"I'm not coming here as a preacher" I reasoned, "I have a six-year-old son. This is material that can be harmful. A pedophile can use this."

"I don't care what you say; we are not doing it." She was unmoved.

In retrospect, I probably would have never done what I did next. I looked at her and then very calmly ripped the book in half.

Then I said, "Now you can call the cops and we'll find out if the DA here in Missouri will prosecute a father and a pastor for ripping up child porn or if they will defend you for selling it."

The lady went irate and called the cops. When they arrived, she lied about what happened and how it happened. I was arrested and was thrown in jail.

They threw me into the "drunk" tank with about eight guys. One of the brothers that went with me also landed in jail. I seized the opportunity to preach to those eight guys. All eight got saved. The brother and I were later bailed out.

That night, we made the news.

According to their story, a preacher tore up a book in Barnes and Noble. But the television station kept blocking out the pictures from the book. That was ironic for a book that they said was not bad!

A news reporter from Crime Stoppers or Action News called me the next day. Someone had just dropped off the book at her desk.

"Pastor Lohrke, I got this book because someone dropped it off at my desk. I'm really appalled at what I'm looking at. Do you have any plans about what you are going to do?"

"Well, that first Barnes and Noble manager promised me that those books would be off the shelf from the other two stores till the DA makes a decision. I'm going over there to see if they have removed them."

"Can I meet you there with my camera?" she asked.

"Absolutely." I said.

My wife, some brothers from church, the news reporter and I showed up at the first Barnes and Noble. When I walked in, they remembered me.

And the books were still on the shelf. I found a manager and, with the book in my hand, said, "Listen, ma'am, I don't know if you know what is going on …"

She interrupted me "I've heard what is going on."

"Listen," I said "I'm just asking that you remove the books until the DA makes a decision."

"Look," she stated, "our stance is that this is art, and we are going to keep this on the shelf."

Knowing that she was not going to move the books I said, "I'll tell you what I'm going to do. I'm going to call the police and have them come."

So I did, except this time, I held onto the book (they had taken the book from me the last time). A police officer responded to my call about child pornography. When he came up to me in front of the news camera, I opened the book in front of his face.

"This is why I'm here." I explained.

"Oh my God!" he said, shocked. "Where did you get that book?"

"I got it right here in Barnes and Noble."

The manager protested. "You did not get that from Barnes and Noble!"

But I was not deterred, "I got it right here. They are selling them."

"Well, that is child porn. That is a no-brainer," the cop concluded. Then he added, "The only thing is that I'm in a situation. The manager has to give this to me. I can't just take the book. I'm a field officer."

Moving toward the manager in front of the camera, I asked her, "Will you please take this book to the police officer so he could take it and look at it?"

"No," she responded.

So I ripped the book.

She yelled, "Officer, arrest that man!"

As the cop handcuffed me, he whispered in my ear, "Man, I was about to rip the book myself."

The cop drove me around the corner before he stopped and removed my handcuffs. He then placed me in the front seat.

"I can't believe what just happened!" he exclaimed. Then he took me down to the precinct.

Whoever is reading this book, please remember this: I am not advocating protests. Never in a million years would I advocate this sort of thing, including protests in front of abortion clinics – I'm not into that kind of stuff. I believe that as we preach the gospel, lives will be changed. This was not premeditated. It was more like righteous indignation.

Police officers greeted me in the parking lot, including women officers who clapped and said, "Good for you. We are glad for you."

They did not throw me in jail this time.

But the story made the news again. Local news stations and even national news stations were calling me, including a syndicated radio show host. He had been discussing the issue on his show.

He called me live on his show and said, "You're my hero."

This started a ripple. Soon, thirty-one cities in the United States had Christians walking into Barnes and Noble and ripping up the same books. Yet none of them were arrested for doing it because the books were porn. It was illegal material. I was the only one thrown in jail for tearing up the book.

Barnes and Nobles responded by putting a front-page article of me in the news and threatening a lawsuit. A Barnes and Noble corporate lawyer from New York even threatened to prosecute me to the full extent of the law. Lawyers from the city where I lived were also calling me wanting to take up the case for free.

Barnes and Noble went a step further — they put up a display in their store about censorship. There was a picture of Adolf Hitler burning books and pictures of other books banned throughout history. Then they added my picture with a picture of the book that I tore up. Ironically, they did not have a picture of the Bible, the most censored book of all time.

The next Sunday, out of nowhere, two hundred people showed up in front of the Barnes and Noble store. They were there to protest. These were Catholics, Baptists, and pastors from other denominations. One church brought their Sunday school kids on a bus and picketed the store saying, "Barnes and Noble exploits children." This got out of hand.

Now I was interviewed on television and radio shows.

I was being clear, "Look, I'm a pastor. I'm not an activist. This just happened. I did this because it's wrong. I did this because of my son. The main thing was I did this because it's illegal. I don't rip up *Playboy* and *Penthouse*. Those are pornography. I don't like them, but they are legal. This was not."

I ended up with two court dates for the arrests. I went to the first court case with my lawyer and the media. On the prosecuting side, the DA was there by himself, but the Barnes and Noble manager was not there, nor was the policeman. Lawyers from Barnes and Noble also failed to show up.

Calling me forward in front of the court, the judge said, "Pastor Lohrke, they did not show up because they are scared of you. They know that if this rules in your favor they are forced to take this book off the shelf. You are doing a good job. Case dismissed."

The next week was my other court case for the second bookstore. On the day before the court case, the judge called my lawyer and said that Barnes and Noble had dropped the charges. Then he suggested that I pick up a copy of *USA Today*. It was headlined, "Barnes and Noble Indicted by Grand Jury for Selling Child Pornography."

Within me was a certain attitude I had as a punk rocker where I went all out for something I believed in – even breaking the law for the devil. That same punk rocker attitude I had now kicked in to fight something I did not think was right. And I was glad for it.

Testing a Heart's Cry

While I was a young convert, I was around radical people.

"Lord," I remembered praying, "if you ever make me a pastor, please give me people that are radical."

He has answered that prayer throughout the years. As far as I know, no one in Kansas City street-preached but our church. Could it be the reason why some people were attracted to us? Possibly. The only people who gave us trouble were Christians. Some of them told us that it was wrong to display Jesus on a cross. But we kept on with our vision.

One Sunday morning, I was preaching a sermon about reaching the lost.

I had just declared, "God, give us the lost. Those that no one else wants!"

Just then, a black guy came roaring in from the back of the church. We had about seventy people in the service. None of my ushers tried to do anything so that the man ran right onto the stage. Reaching out, I grabbed him by the neck and he was growling. Behind him followed two cops. I urged the church to pray for this man as I held him in a firm grip. He was so filthy and dirty with an awful smell that when I took my hand off him, it was dirty. The two cops who had followed the man were talking at the back of the church talking and then they left. Later I found out that the police had seen him doing something suspicious at a gas station. They chased him all the way to our church.

But when the cops saw me they said, "Well, there's that one preacher that is always there. I guess he has everything under control." And they left him there.

I had the man sit in the front row. Toward the end of the service, he headed for the restroom. This was nothing unusual. Besides, we had people there and I was preoccupied with ministering. Concluding the service, I stayed and talked to the people until the last of them left – except for the ushers, I thought.

It had been quite a service. Sitting in my office afterward, I was thinking about what happened when an usher came and said, "Hey, that guy is still in the bathroom."

"What is he doing?"

"I don't know." The usher was puzzled. "He won't open the door."

"How long has he been in there?" I asked.
"About forty minutes."

"Are you kidding me? Get him out of there!"

The usher was not the aggressive type. "I don't know what to do," he said.

"Well, let me show you what we do in LA."

I pounded on the door and the man hollered from the inside, "What?"

"Open this door, man!" I yelled back. "I'm going to kick this door down if you don't get out of my bathroom."

He opened the door and he was butt naked. He had taken my toilet apart so that water was shooting up from the pipe and he was taking a bath and washing his clothes. Water was all over the floor and disappearing into the floor drain. I could not believe what I was seeing.

"Dude, get your clothes on!" I said.

Afterward, we prayed with him and took him down to the men's home.

This was the kind of crazy things that happened at my church. When you say that you want to reach the lost, you will be tested on this. Sometimes though, when people say they want to reach the lost, they mean the fish that has been cleaned up and filleted. But someone has to get the dirty fish.

Turning Point

I got into a rut. Being a pastor for about five years, I got into a routine, the same old, same old. Sincere but there was no freedom. My wife was leading songs. This was a real turning point for the church.

It was a Wednesday night and we had forty or fifty people. By tradition, we sang for thirty to forty minutes, and afterward I would traditionally get the microphone at the last song. Prayer usually followed, then came the offering and after that the announcements. Everything was like clockwork.

When I walked up to take the microphone from Esther, I fell out under the power of God and became slain in the spirit. God struck me. Immediately, I was weeping and crying. Since I came from a Pentecostal Charismatic background, I thought that I would go with this because God was touching me. I had landed where my head was turned to the back of the stage and I could not see anyone in the church. After a while, I decided to get up. I tried but couldn't because it felt like someone was sitting on me. Still aware of what was going on around (I could hear the piano playing), I was speaking in tongues and saying, "God, I've got to go." But I could not get up. This went on for forty-five minutes.

In my mind as a pastor I talked to the Lord "God what about the offering? We need an offering. I got to preach a sermon."

Right then, I felt the Holy Spirit who said, "Give me back my church."

The words of Philippians 3:10 came to mind, "That I may know Him and the power of His resurrection." God began to deal with me about His church.

He said, "I want freedom in this house of worship."

After this long period of time where the Lord had me pinned down like a wrestler on TV, I felt a release in my neck and I was able to turn around and look at my church. There I was worried about them, but when I looked out, I saw that everyone was laid out in the spirit. They were weeping and crying and the power of God fell in that place.

At that very moment, I decided that we were going to have fun and we were going to be flexible. If we were worshipping and it was time to stop, we would stop. If the offering had to wait to be taken at the end, then that was what we would do. We were going to let God have His way. Such freedom was in our services after that decision. Lives began to get touched and changed.

About a month later, a prophet came to preach for us who moved in the prophetic gifting. This was the first time he came to preach for us. This revival was nothing like I had ever seen before. He was ministering and calling out people, praying and prophesying over them. The result of that revival was an increased number of weddings and new converts in our local body. Though the meetings were meant to be for a few days, they went on for two weeks. I was excited and blown away at what God was doing. Our numbers doubled. Toward the end of that revival, we decided that the storefront was not big enough for us.

****

Taking Off the Limits on God

Psalm 78 revealed how God's people, the Israelites limited Him (verse 41). They held back God through unbelief. Those who died in the desert limited God in their life and what He could do. Imagine, they could have gone all the way to the Promised Land and defeated all the giants!

Don't limit God in your life. Let Him use you to the full extent because one day when we stand before God, it will be worth it all. We will receive a crown and a reward. Then all the trials and the pains of this life will pale in the light of those rewards.

God wants to use the church as His vehicle to express His power against the enemy. He gave us that power to tear down strongholds and dominions. That always challenged me. The church should be a church that fights, not just singing and having programs. We are meant to pull down the walls of darkness and take back souls from the enemy. Jesus has already won and has put all things under His feet (Ephesians 1:22). He conquered death, the grave and the enemy. We have His heart and boldness.

****

More Paradigm Shifts

A new and bigger building meant another storefront. You see, I was taught that we didn't own buildings — we rent them. This was another paradigm that God had to break in my mind.

One day, Esther and I took a new route home from church. We drove down a different street just one block over from our church. There was a very large church for sale almost with the same address on that street.

My wife exclaimed, "That's our church! That's our church!"

But my response was similar to when she said that it was God's will for us to go to Kansas City. Then, I had told her that I prayed way more than her.

This time I said, "You don't know what you're talking about. That church probably costs all kinds of money. We have a small budget. They'll never sell to us."

She insisted that she had the same feeling she had when she felt that we had to come to Kansas. That shook me up and I got the hint.

We called about the property. I remembered calling a bond place and trying to get a loan. At that time, we barely had eighty people in the church we had no equity, and we could not get a loan. I made a decision to sell my house in order to get it. Next door to the church was a parsonage and I volunteered to move my family there. The sacrifice paid off, because we got a loan for $500,000 to get the building.

There was not much privacy at the parsonage. People were coming knocking on my door at all hours of the night, even some from off the street. News had gotten around that a pastor lived there. Some of them were on drugs and were asking for money or needing prayer. Disciples were bringing demon-possessed people to my front yard. They said, "Pastor, pray for them."

"You pray for them," I told them. "I want to go to bed."

But the move to get the building proved to be a good one. I'll never forget how exciting that was.

When we moved into the building two monumental things took place.

We had an open revival with my friend Rob Sanchez. Our planned three-day revival continued for five weeks. Church services happened every single day, and we could not stop it if we wanted to because the place was instantly packed. We had three hundred salvations and five weddings during those meetings. People got saved that were living in sin and wanted to get married right away. We were marrying them right in service. It was a sovereign move of God. This thing was taking on a life of its own.

Following the six-week revival was the production of the drama *Hell Night*. We had always done this drama before, but this time, we had the means to make it into a big deal. This was basically the white throne drama we performed way back in San Francisco in that little church before I married Esther.

Kansas City is famous for haunted houses. There is a district there with old warehouses. Everyone came from the tri-state area and paid $20 to see these haunted houses. They were a big attraction. Why not present the drama about the big white throne judgment showing heaven and hell on a big scale?

When we first did this drama at the radio station, there were a few people that were involved in it. Hell was just a black sheet with a lamp from my bedroom. We took the lampshade off and if someone went to hell, they would start screaming behind the black sheet and they'd rub their fingers behind the light. The shadow of their fingers was on the ceiling and they were screaming, "Help me Jesus, we should have gone to church!" We had all these characters from different walks of life who were judged and some went to hell and others to heaven.

Again, we had done the drama at the State Avenue church, our prior location. The drama seemed like it was the only thing that was doing good for us. Up to that point, the biggest crowd we had for Hell Night was a couple of 100 people and about 80 people received salvation. That was exciting to us.

But we were in for a surprise. The first time we had the drama at the new church, we had about a thousand people show up. Our church seated only five hundred people! We did the drama three times a night. And over a period of seven nights, we had ten thousand people show up. That first year, seventeen hundred people came up to accept Christ as Savior. I did not know what to do, and I was not even doing two services. The first Sunday after the drama, we had no room for people and I had to turn them away.

I said, "Oh my gosh. What is going on here? I don't even have a plan for this."

Every year since, we have done that drama and we have not had a year where we had less than two thousand people get saved. The last time we did that play, we had twenty-three thousand people saved in a matter of seven packed out nights. People have lined up at my church at three in the afternoon all the way till seven at night waiting for to see it. I was doing altar calls at one o'clock in the morning.

What I loved about this drama is that most churches do the traditional dramas about Easter and Christmas. This was a tough drama. There was nothing nice about it except for Jesus. It was targeting non-Christians a hundred percent. It was graphic. It was edgy. It dealt with so many things. Of course we got persecuted. I remembered that I put some commercials on television for it the second year.

The guy at the television station asked me, "So your church is Praise Chapel. What religious program do you want your commercials on?"

"Put it on Jerry Springer, Howard Stern and some kind of dating shows," I said, "I want them on the raunchiest shows you have. Please put them with wrestling or something like that."

The guy thought I was crazy.

But those were the kind of people who came. They were lost.

Recently after the drama, I had gone down to the church for prayer. It's Saturday morning and I was at prayer and the Lord instructed me to drive down to this property off the freeway. Fourteen acres of land were for sale. I knew the amount they were asking for this property (about $900,000 or one million). Also, I knew that they had plans to put a strip mall there with a gas station and a convenient store. But I went and stood there at the property, trying to feel it out and obey God.

I called the real estate agent, "Hey, I'm a pastor and I'm here at the property. I'm inquiring about it."

The agent said, "Well, you need to confirm. There are plans to build on this property. The contractor has not fulfilled his contract. As a matter of fact, his contract is up but the contractor is going to renew it."

I said, "Well, I'm just inquiring about it."

"Well, it's funny that you called today," the agent continued. "The owner died today. And he was a friend that I've known for years and have done stuff with his family."

"Wow!" I said, "I'm so sorry. Would you just please tell the widow, his wife, that the church will be saying a prayer for her family. We are sorry about it. Let her know that the church inquired."

Three weeks later, I received a call from the real estate agent, "Pastor Lohrke, you are not going to believe this but I told the widow that you called and you checked. She does not want to deal with the developer anymore. She was honored that you were interested and wanted to put a church there. She had some tax issues and she said, "You know what? You tell that church if they want to buy the property, we will sell it to them for $300,000."

That is the property that we are now in the process of building our forty-thousand-square-foot building on, which will seat a thousand people. That is our goal.

CHAPTER FIVE

Going Places

Around the World

Mexico was my training ground for missions. Once a place where I went to for a good time, it became the place to train me for ministering overseas. Traveling to minister there was always exciting. Doors were opening for me to travel to different countries to minister the gospel.

My first mission trip overseas as a pastor was with my two best friends, Pastor Abraham and Pastor Ronnie Chavez. Because of all the places we had to visit, our trip was three weeks long. We preached in Nicaragua for a week, then Honduras, Costa Rica and ended up in Cuba. Preaching crusades on the street, doing revival meetings and conferences were exciting. We began to realize that churches and people around the world just want someone to come and preach. Other places I ended up traveling to were the Philippines, Amsterdam, then Ghana and Kenya (Pastor Joseph Yamatutu).

Perhaps the most memorable visit I had was to Ghana, Africa, to preach for Pastor Frank Donker. It was an outdoor crusade. People were getting healed and saved. While sitting there on a wooden plank platform behind the stage praying, the reality of it all hit me — I was a punker and there I was preaching in a foreign land!

Down on my knees I went as I cried and said to the Lord, "God, how did I end up here on the other side of the world? I'm just a punk rocker in the garage that you saved and look where you have taken me, Jesus." What a humbling experience! I was emotional as I was humbly reminded of what God could do in a life.

****

Sent Out or Went Out

One thing needs to be understood. I was blessed to have my pastor send me out to pastor a church. Jesus sent out the apostles and disciples. Peter and the other apostles laid hands on them and sent them out. There is a difference between went and sent. Many people will go out of emotion or feeling without covering or direction. But the Bible talked about release or being sent, though the Lord will use anyone who will preach. That is the most effective and Biblical way.

Everything you read in this book showed how I was raised up in a crazy world and how God used that tenacity and zeal for His glory. Moses was trained as a military leader and learned leadership skills in the land of Egypt. He was raised in Pharaoh's house and was not an ignorant man but a well-versed one. Then God called him. He was able to guide a few million people out of Egypt into the Promised Land.

God will use our past experiences for His favor and purposes. The Apostle Paul's training as a zealous and violent Pharisee was used by God to spread the Gospel. He thought he was doing things for God when he wasn't at first. Salvation did not take away Paul's zeal for what he believed in; he was just as crazy. Much has to do with a Bible Study leader, the pastor, a church and a fellowship that believed in people.

I could have landed anywhere but I thank God that He put me in that Praise Chapel church. They believed that God had a plan for anyone no matter what their financial situation, their looks or their skin color. God can use anyone. It was a place where people were genuinely glad when you got saved. It was a very unselfish place. It was a place where they were excited when people were sent out. I could have easily ended up in a place where they kept everything inside, a place where only a few get to minister. Praise Chapel was a place where I was able to be involved. God used my training and involvement in the dramas, outreaches and Bible Studies while in Praise Chapel, to help me pioneer a church.

A punk rocker is all I was – a sinner saved by Grace. I never want to forget where I came from. If I forget I might get arrogant, religious and prideful. I want to stay humble.

****

About four hundred people were present for a crusade in the trash field in Kenya. We were praying for miracles. My church too was praying and fasting for miracles to take place in this crusade. Through an interpreter, I was preaching about hope and healing. People were getting healed but they were not major healings.

At the end of the night, a lady brought up a girl. The interpreter said that the girl was deaf.

I said, "Bring her here on the stage."

She was born deaf and had never spoken in her life. There is a big difference between not hearing well and never having heard. All the things I was taught about believing God for healing and miracles was on the line. Even the words I heard as a disciple came to mind.

Pastor Neville had said, "Go for it! God is going to use all of our lives. Lay hands on the sick and they will recover. Believe God; don't doubt Him! Pray for the sick!"

I told myself, "This is it!"

So I laid hands on her and prayed for a miracle. I prayed once and nothing happened. Twice, nothing happened. Third time, her ears lit up. She was now responding to the sounds, even standing from afar. But she still could not speak. Faith arose in that place. We began to pray that God would loosen her tongue.

"Jesus!" I said out loud.

The young girl yelled out, "Jesus!" Then she cried, "Mommy" and then she said, "Pastor Kelly!"

About that time, people started running from the streets. Then it got crazy. I was getting nervous as people were coming from all over. Everyone in that area knew that girl. And this was at the end of the night.

On the following night, we had two thousand people standing there. I prayed and made a commitment to lay hands on everyone in that dirt field. People were getting healed and delivered from demonic possession. It was a marvelous experience. While standing there behind that little wooden stage made of pieces of wood with a string of lights, I was praying and thinking about God's goodness in my life.

"Lord, the things you have done!" I said in my heart, "I was not supposed to live or make it. I almost died of an overdose several times." But there I was used by God to reach people in a different nation. That was God's doing.

No one thought of me as anything but God thought something of me. I am still a young man (forty-one is young) and am able to serve the Lord for many more years. My heart's desire is to finish the course and stay saved. Not just to stay saved but to stay on fire for God and keep a passion for Him. At the end of my life, I want to know that I was not disobedient to what God had set out for me.

****

Forever Zealous

One of my favorite stories is in the book of Acts (Acts 26). Paul is before King Agrippa and Paul is on trial for his own life. He shared the story of how God touched him. He told of how God shone a bright light and blinded him and knocked him off his horse. Then he heard the voice of God call him into the ministry. God was going to use him to reach the Gentiles and open their eyes to the truth (verse 18).

King Agrippa, who had the power to sentence Paul to death, heard Paul proclaim the gospel. That did not intimidate Paul. He was not afraid to witness to someone years later in his life. King Agrippa said that Paul almost persuaded him to be a Christian. This is a challenge – to be as excited as he was about Jesus as the day he was first saved.

Paul had plenty of opportunities to witness to Christians, but now he was witnessing to nonbelievers. He was hoping that everyone that heard him would become a Christian. Paul preached bold and loud, even toward the end of his life. He fought the good fight and ran the race.

At the end of my life, my prayer is that I was not disobedient to what God has for me. The challenge is from Hebrews where it says to lay aside all weight and run the race with endurance (Hebrews 12:1). Paul was fanatical. He never lost his zeal for God. He was excited and crazy for God. He said he was not mad (Acts 26:25). He spoke the truth. Paul was convinced that he knew the truth.

Can we still witness to someone years later and possess the same zeal that we had when we first got saved? Keep your sword sharp. Share the gospel. Though people know that you are a pastor, can you still witness to a waiter or waitress after service on Sunday? It is one thing to preach to Christians and it is another thing to witness to nonbelievers.

****

Till I See Jesus…

This story began with a mailman named Bobby who had a dream and believed God enough to pick up the phone to call my grandpa. Through a series of events I ended up at the garage and got saved. For that, I am forever grateful. That mailman went from Fresno, California, to Puerto Rico as a minister, then to the Dominican Republic and then to Dallas, Texas. Two years ago, after Bobby had lived in Dallas, Texas, for fourteen years, he went on a forty-day fast and felt God told him to spend the rest of his life overseas in the old Soviet Union. He now lives in Estonia, desiring to go into Poland and Romania and other such countries with the gospel of Jesus. At his age, he's not looking to retire but to do something continuous for God.

I want to finish strong and not finish because I retired. I am not giving up or passing the torch to someone else. This is not referring to discipleship where you have to leave something for someone. This is more of a desire to die doing God's will.

Going from a "punker to pastor," my attitude remains the same – Give it your all! The only difference is that I went from a life of sin to a life of righteousness. In my punker years, I gave sin and Satan my all and held nothing back. Should I offer my Lord Jesus any less? My desire within these pages is to truly challenge every reader to give the Lord Jesus Christ their all, and not to hold anything back; be radical in their service to God. Clearly, if we could live a life of radical sin, why not live one of radical obedience? Saul killed Christians in a hardcore manner and destroyed lives, until his encounter with Jesus changed him. Then he became hardcore for Jesus. He then lived a radical life inflicting pain in the kingdom of darkness. Paul had a hardcore punk rock attitude that I love about Christianity.

We must live our lives and fulfill all that God has for us. As my Pastor Mike Neville used to say, "Go for it!" This is the attitude that will make a difference in the world that we live in. We have one life to live and only a certain amount of time to live it. We have wasted plenty of time before, living for our selves, and now we must give it all to Christ. God can take any life and mold, shape and then build it to be used by Him.

****

Praise Chapel

Praise Chapel was a church formed in 1976 by Pastor Neville. He was twenty-eight-years-old when he was asked to take over an all-white church. The church dwindled to a small core. He realized that the church did not reflect the neighborhood. He wanted to reach everyone with the gospel and so he preached that way and reached out in that community. The church grew to about a thousand as Hispanics, drug dealers and prostitutes were saved. Today, Praise Chapel is a fellowship of about two hundred churches world-wide.

www.praisechapel.com

APPENDIX

Mom's Side of the Story (In Her Own Words)

Hope for the Hopeless

The context of my memories are not necessarily in chronological order. There are thoughts that came to me while flashing back and forth in time. It was very difficult for me to dredge up these painful memories. Past-life description: single mother, working with my own life in turmoil. I was impatient, fearful and dealing with my own demons. Latchkey kid. Father in and out of life. Always grandparents present. Kelly's grandparents worshiped him. Grandparents loving influence in both our lives. I took a day off work and went on a helicopter to Ports of Call. We enjoyed a wonderful day in Disneyland and had a wonderful time. We experienced a lot of wonderful times together, including a Hawaiian vacation for his sixth grade graduation. In earlier times, I would work ten to twelve hours a day. We would take his various friends with us on our vacations and outings. During the tumultuous times, I was also dealing with my mom's mental illness.

At the age of twelve, out of desperation, I sent Kelly to live with his father for a few months. Then one day, his father told me to grant him full custody or take him away. Kelly did not want to be with his father full time. After his return, it was evident that he was on drugs. I suspected marijuana usage. I had a place for him in therapy, including seven months in rehab. Unbeknownst to anyone at the time, a counselor was giving out pot. Kelly broke out of lockdown along with a friend and two days later they were found at a friend's place.

He was taken back to rehab in a mellow state. Within two months of being released, Kelly was worse than ever. He got into high school on a prayer of loved ones. While playing on the basketball team, his grades were poor. He was removed from the team. He returned to his troublesome friends and became problematic. My house was a gathering place for him and his drug-using friends while I was at work. Any food I had purchased was eaten by him and his friends leaving my house in a disaster. They ran up my phone bill with 900 numbers.

At fourteen and fifteen, Kelly would disappear for days at a time. At home, he would just sleep. After the problems at Downey High, he went to continuation school. He could not be helped even when a teacher provided transportation. Kelly was arrested for curfew violation. At fifteen, he was a drug runner to San Francisco. Somewhere during that time, I received a call from the police that Kelly's friends had stolen property and a gun and had hidden it in my home. Kelly gave the gun to a friend. I hired a lawyer. Kelly was placed on probation. He hung out in Hollywood with a life of sex and drugs.

When he was sixteen, I came home from work with the news of his grandpa's passing. His grandpa loved him more than life itself. He wrote to Kelly that he continuously prayed for him. Towing the line on his probation, Kelly had to meet with his probation officer on the day of the funeral. Also during this time, Kelly swallowed a lot of pills and then took off. He came back and I took him to the hospital to have his stomach pumped. The death of his grandpa sent him out of control. It was hell on earth.

His friends would climb in the window at all hours ransacking the house (Some of his friends would steal stuff and wait for Kelly to get them pawned). Kelly would put holes in the walls or hit me and left me fearing for my life. The phone would constantly ring for him and I was unable to use the phone for anything. His friends were punk rockers. I even found marijuana growing on my roof. I would come home to one tattoo after another. That made me sick. Then there was the Mohawk haircut and ear piercings. Kelly would get odd jobs but would be so out of control that he would hit me if he did not like what I said or did. It brought back flashback memories of my life when his father was abusing me.

It got so bad that I had to sell my home and move out of the neighborhood out of embarrassment because his friends were constantly arriving. I hid in Lakewood apartments in fear for my life. Kelly informed me later that he would go with his friends to smoke pot. At this point I had to kick him out and he moved into a place in Woodier. He had a job and his grandmother and I would take him food. After moving from Whittier, he asked his grandfather on his father's side if he could rent the garage apartment. He was invited to a Bible Study. He even asked me for different clothes so he could shed his rocker image, so which I happily bought him a new wardrobe.

After a while, Kelly met Esther and his life turned around.

BANDS THAT I WENT TO SEE:

1. Pil
2. Social Distortion
3. The Vandals
4. The Damned
5. Dead Kennedys
6. X
7. Youth Brigade
8. Circle One
9. Exploited
10. Bad Religion
11. Shattered Faith
12. Angry Samoans
13. Redd Kross
14. The Dickies
15. Suicidal Tendencies
16. The Exploited
17. GPH
18. Fear
19. DOA
20. Bad Brains
21. Misfits
22. Black Flag
23. The Mentors
24. MDC

CLUBS THAT I FREQUENTED

1. Fenders
2. Olympic Auditorium
3. Café de Grande of Hollywood
4. Santa Monica Civic Center
5. Madame Wong's
6. Devonshire Downs
7. Anti-club
8. Mendiol's Ballroom

REFERENCES

*Footnotes included explanation of names and terms from www.wikipedia.org and www.medterms.com.